Modern LOCOMOTIVES ILLUSTRATED

Annual No. 2

Modern LOCOMOTIVES ILLUSTRATED

Annual No. 2

Compiled by Colin J. Marsden &
Christopher G. Perkins

TheRailwayCentre.Com
Publishing

First published 2010

ISBN 978-0-9557887-5-8

PO Box 45, Dawlish, Devon. EX7 9XY

Code: 1010/C

Visit The Railway Centre.Com website at www.therailwaycentre.com

Half Title: *A train which always makes people stop and look is the British Royal Train. Kept at Wolverton under strict security, the claret liveried stock operates between 15-20 special services each year transporting HM The Queen or Prince Charles to engagements. Early on the morning of 11 March 2010 the full Royal set powered by Class 67 No. 67006, with coaches 2920, 2915, 2917, 2923, 2904, 2903, 2921 and No. 67005 on the rear pass Dawlish as the 09.15 Newton Abbot Hackney Yard to Exeter conveying Her Majesty the Queen to Exeter.* Colin J. Marsden

Title: *The ever changing railway scene, few would have thought when this image was recorded on 8 October 2002 that the Class 442 'Wessex Electric' sets would be ousted from the South West Trains network and by 2010 be operating on the Gatwick Express service. In this view we see set No. 442408 departing from Bincombe Tunnel near journeys end while forming the 11.30 Waterloo-Weymouth.* Colin J. Marsden

Front Cover: *Traversing the Highland Main Line at Slochd, DRS Class 37 No. 37611 and Class 66/4 No. 66432 power train 4N47, the 13.10 Inverness to Grangemouth 'Stobart' train on 30 May 2009. The Class 66 had previously failed with a TPWS defect and required to be piloted.* Neil Gibson

Back Cover Top: *One of the hot spots for rail activity in the diesel hydraulic era was Newton Abbot, where a sizeable depot, workshop and carriage sidings existed adjacent to the four platform station, which was a hive of activity. This is a view of the station area with the depot and works on the right, taken from a bridge at the west end, and shows 'Western' No. D1012 Western Firebrand in pristine condition leading train 1C60, the 14.30 Paddington to Penzance on 28 April 1971. Today Newton Abbot is just a shadow of its former self, with only three platforms and no sidings.* Bernard Mills

Back Cover Middle: *In pristine condition English Electric Type 4 No. D384 painted in 1960s BR green with a small yellow warning panel, passes Roade Junction Signal Box (located behind the locomotive) at 07.00 on 1 July 1964 powering Royal Special 1X01 from Edinburgh Princes Street to London Euston, conveying HM The Queen and other members of the Royal Household. Note the cable on the front of the loco which connected to the Royal stock to provide voice communication between train and locomotive.* Robin Patrick

Back Cover Bottom: *Today the standard diesel locomotive motive power for the Fenland area is the Class 66. On 23 May 2007 EWS now DBS No. 66082 powers one of the daily Mountsorrel (Leicestershire) to Kennet stone trains, formed of four-wheel PGA type hoppers. The train is seen near Manea.* Michael J. Collins

Below: *In 2009-10 the first six General Electric type JPH37ACmi locos have entered traffic with Freightliner on both Heavy Haul and Intermodal services. The locos are classified 70 under TOPS. No. 70003 heads away from Westerleigh Junction past Ram Hill powering train 4Z70 from Rugeley Power Station to Stoke Gifford Yard formed of empty high-capacity hoppers on 4 March 2010.* Chris Perkins

Introduction

Welcome to *Modern Locomotives Illustrated Annual No. 2*. As with Annual No. 1 we have covered a broad spectrum of the modern traction railway scene which would not normally be covered by our *Modern Locomotives Illustrated* magazine. There are sections looking at railway routes and specific rail operations, such as the Cornish china clay traffic and Network Rail's varied fleet of locomotives and coaching stock, which should assist the modeller with these interesting vehicles. As with the first *MLI* Annual, we have included material on overseas railways which includes some of Europe's top photographic locations described by overseas rail expert Philip Wormald.

We strive to obtain the highest production quality and in order to obtain this we use the very best original material and production equipment available.

All images for the Annuals and *MLI* magazines are processed using Adobe CS4 software on Apple computers using the settings and profiles to match the Ian Allan production and printing department.

It is our intention to publish *MLI* Annual No. 3 at the end of 2011 and we already have ideas on subjects for inclusion. However we would be very pleased to hear from anybody who may have suitable photographic or written material for an article.

The Railway Centre.Com Ltd, the publishers of *Modern Locomotives Illustrated* are always interested to either borrow or purchase original colour material of the older classes of modern traction. If you have any that you wish to dispose of please contact the editorial team.

We hope that you will enjoy reading this latest edition of the *MLI* Annual and we are already enjoying working on the next edition.

Colin J. Marsden
Christopher G. Perkins

A limited number of copies of *Modern Locomotives Illustrated Annual No. 1* are still available at just £17.99 post free from the publishers, TRC Publishing.Com Ltd, PO Box 45, Dawlish, Devon, EX7 9XY or call the order hot line on 01626 862320.

Subjects covered in MLI Annual No. 1 are - Dealing with Winter Snow; ● West Coast over the Fells; ● Electric to Shanklin; ● Rails to Slovenia; ● West Highland Class 37s; ● The Class 501/97 Story; ● Doncaster 'Plant' Works; ● The Derby 'Mag-Lev'; ● California Passenger Action; ● Oils to Westerleigh; ● North East Class 56 Action; ● Working the 'Water Cannon'; ● First Generation DMMUs; ● Export Brush Type 4s; ● Preservation Masterclass.

Contents

The Settle & Carlisle Line

By Chris Perkins

The Settle & Carlisle route opened for traffic between August 1875 and April 1876 being the last mainline railway built in England.

The Midland Railway wanted it's own route to Scotland, having prior to depend on its rival the London & North Western Railway to reach Carlisle, who were often obstructive. The only way was via the 'roof of England' over the Pennine Hills as the earlier routes north had taken the easier course to the west and east.

A Bill of Parliament was granted in 1866 for the construction of the line, but the directors and shareholders of the Midland Railway became concerned over the estimated cost of the project and, due to the economic situation in the country at the time, they applied to have the Bill withdrawn. In April 1869 permission was granted and construction of the line started later that year. The 72 mile line took six years to construct becoming one of the most difficult and expensive railway projects attempted in Britain, and eventually costing three and a half million pounds. Over 5,000 men were employed on the project, many of whom lost their lives due to the very harsh conditions they worked and lived under with at least 80 persons, many of them children, dying of smallpox in the Batty Green encampment at the Ribblehead site.

The line, engineered by John Crossley was designed for use by express passenger trains and, in an effort to keep curves and gradients to a minimum; some major earthworks and structures were required over most of the route. The steepest gradient was kept to 1:100 but this meant 16 miles of continuous climb from Settle to Blea Moor tunnel with most of it at the ruling gradient which became known to enginemen as 'The Long Drag'. The outcome of this supposed easier route meant the construction of 14 tunnels and 22 viaducts including the famous Ribblehead viaduct at 1,320 ft long and 104 ft high, and many of the stations were some considerable distance from the villages after which they were named.

Following the 1923 merger between the London & North Western Railway and the Midland Railway, the route was at a severe disadvantage over the West Coast Main Line which was not only shorter but had fewer operating difficulties. The 1963 Beeching report recommended that the passenger services should be withdrawn from the line and although this did not happen at the time, in 1970 apart from Settle and Appleby, all stations were closed and just two passenger trains each way a day served the route.

During the summer of 1974, Dales Rail services were run on weekends to some of the closed stations to enable ramblers access to the area. These trains were promoted by the Yorkshire National Park Authority and the promotional literature at the time asked passengers not to arrive at stations more than 30 minutes prior to departure of their train as the station areas were private property.

After the electrification of the West Coast Main Line in 1975, the Thames-Clyde Express finished running and most other traffic was diverted away resulting in a long period of lack of investment for the route. In the early 1980s the line was carrying very little traffic and British Rail had decided that due to low traffic figures and the high cost of maintaining the infrastructure, the line would have to close and a period of closure by stealth set in.

In 1981 the Friends of the Settle-Carlisle Line (FoSCL) was formed to protest against the closure even though this had not been officially announced. The official closure notice finally came in 1984 with British Rail claiming that the repair of Ribblehead viaduct alone would cost between £6 and 8 million. From the campaign that followed, and a very positive contribution by the then Minister of State for Transport, Michael Portillo, the line was eventually saved and having been so much in the public eye passenger journeys increased from around 93,000 in 1983 to 450,000 in 1989 and are currently around 750,000. The repair to Ribblehead viaduct was eventually completed within budget for less than £3.25 million and eight of the stations were re-opened.

Currently the route is probably as busy as it has ever been and there are 15 booked freight paths in daylight hours although many of these are run 'as required' and, following a recent visit to the line, there were certainly more running at night than during the day. Most of these workings are loaded coal trains between Scotland and English power stations and returning empties. There are six passenger trains each way with one being a semi-fast service calling at Settle, Kirkby Stephen and Appleby only, Monday to Friday. There is also an evening service from Leeds that terminates at Ribblehead. There is one extra train on Saturdays but only four run on Sundays.

Passenger trains are operated by Northern Rail and normally formed of Class 158 units for the winter timetable and a pair during the summer months, but Class 153 and 156 units can also be seen.

Investment continues to be made on the line to cope with this heavy additional traffic and 2010 has seen further welded rail installed. There is even talk of putting the double track back over Ribblehead viaduct.

Many of the stations have been restored to their former Midland Railway glory and all are extremely well looked after. Settle and Kirkby Stephen both have shops where limited refreshments can be obtained; Ribblehead has a museum and visitor centre while Dent, along with the adjacent 'snow huts', has been turned into holiday accommodation.

The spectacular scenery and impressive engineering works on the line continue to draw the enthusiast to enjoy it whatever the season. ∎

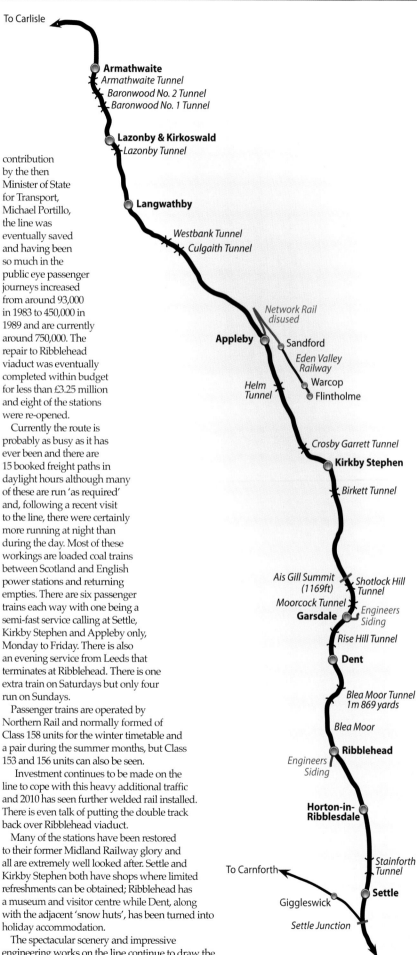

© TRC 2010

Above: On 23 March 2003, Class 57/3 No. 57304 **Gordon Tracy** *crosses Ais Gill viaduct on the final part of the climb to the summit with a diverted West Coast Main Line service, the 12.16 Glasgow Central to London Euston.* Neil Gibson

Below: *Freightliner Class 66/5 No. 66553 has just passed over the summit and is dropping down grade towards Ais Gill viaduct on 23 March 2003 forming the 14.00 York Holgate Yard to Carlisle Yard empty coal service.* Neil Gibson

Above: *On a crisp snowy 7 January 2010, Class 66/0 No. 66065 slogs up grade past Appleby North signal box with a loaded Hunterston to Drax power station coal train.* Imagerail.com

Left: *Class 25s Nos. 25104 and 25142 climb northbound past Selside on 4 September 1981 with loaded 'Presflo' cement hoppers from Clitheroe.* Imagerail.com

Below: *The modern version of the above train, the 6M00, the 07.03 Mossend to Clitheroe empty cement tanks is powered by Class 66/0 No. 66118 and has just crossed Ribblehead viaduct and approaches Ribblehead station on 20 April 2009.* Neil Gibson

Above: On 2 September 1981, Class 47/4 No. 47478 powers a Glasgow to Nottingham service past Blea Moor signal box with what was a standard train formation for the time - seven Mk1s. The scene here has changed little over the years. Imagerail.com

Below: Slightly further north, and looking in the opposite direction to the above photograph, this view shows the barren area around Blea Moor and Ribblehead. With Pen-y-ghent dominating the background, Class 60 No. 60094 **Tryfan** heads the 04.46 Drax Power Station to Kirby Thore loaded gypsum train towards Blea Moor tunnel on 2 June 1997. David Stacey

Above: *The Settle & Carlisle line has been a very popular route for railtours over the years, originally for steam charters but it now also has its fair share of modern traction charters as illustrated by this Spitfire Railtour from Sheffield to Edinburgh on 27 September 2008, powered by West Coast Railway Class 37s Nos. 37248 and 37712. The train is seen approaching Garsdale station from the south, this is a short level section in the climb to Ais Gill, and in the steam era was the site of Garsdale water troughs which were at the highest altitude in the world.* Richard Armstrong

Below: *The diverted 1S63 from London Euston to Glasgow Central is powered by Class 57/3 'Thunderbird' No. 57313* **Tracy Island** *formed of a Class 390 'Pendolino' set and is recorded passing over Sheriff Brow viaduct spanning the River Ribble on 28 April 2007. This was one of the occasions that West Coast Main Line services were diverted via the Settle & Carlisle to allow engineering work on the main line.* Richard Armstrong

Above: *On a perfect Settle & Carlisle day with deep fresh snow and blue sky, Class 66/5 No. 66544 nears the summit at Ais Gill with the 04.38 Killoch to Ratcliffe Power Station loaded coal train on 6 January 2010. Wild Boar Fell dominates the background.* John Longden

Below: *The Kirkby Thore to Milford sidings empty gypsum container train has just crossed the 12 arch Dandry Mire viaduct and is seen approaching Garsdale station powered by DBS Class 66/0 No. 66134 on 19 March 2009. This location was formerly known as Hawes Junction with the branch to Hawes heading off to the right. Above the signal can be seen Hawes Junction Chapel which opened in the same year as the railway in 1876.* John Longden

Above: *The current form of traction over the S&C line is portrayed here with Class 158 No. 158790 in Rugby League Challenge Cup vinyls, passing Selside Shaw forming the 14.00 Carlisle to Leeds on 3 October 2008.* Scott Borthwick

Left: *On 2 January 2010, Northern Class 158 No. 158787 approaches Dent station, near the site of Dent signal box, forming the 10.49 Leeds to Carlisle.* Chris Perkins

Below: *DRS Class 66/4 No. 66427 has just emerged from Moorcock tunnel, crossed Lunds viaduct and past under Grisedale crossing footbridge with spent ballast from a possession at Clitheroe to Carlisle Yard on 16 June 2008.* John Longden

Above: *On 16 June 2008, Class 220 and Class 221 'Voyagers' form a southbound diverted WCML service through Mallerstang Common at Angerholme.* John Longden

Right: *On 9 February 2006 a Freightliner Class 66 crosses Arten Gill viaduct with the 08.25 New Cummock to Drax power station loaded coal hoppers.* Neil Gibson

Below: *Between October 2003 and September 2004 Arriva Trains Northern used 'top & tailed' Class 37/4s with Mk 2 stock on a S&C diagram. The penultimate Carlisle to Leeds service on 24 September 2004 passes Waitby with spruced up No. 37411 leading and No. 37408 on the rear.* Richard Armstrong

Above: *Having dropped off some intrepid fell walkers at Dent, Class 158 No. 158853 forming the 09.00 Leeds to Carlisle departs and passes over Monkey Beck on 2 January 2010. Compared with the picture below, the station buildings have been restored including a new waiting shelter on the 'up' platform. The main building is now a luxury holidey let.* **Chris Perkins**

Left Middle: *On 3 September 1981 Class 47 No. 47478 heads a Nottingham to Glasgow service through Dent station. There is a general air of dereliction compared with the current scene. The signal box has closed and awaiting demolition and the signal posts are devoid of arms.* **Imagerail.com**

Left Below: *Class 66/0 No. 66205 heads through Dent station on 9 February 2006 with the 05.00 Hunterston to Eggborough Power Station. Even some 30 years after the removal of the signals, the painted sighting panel still remains on the Coal Road overbridge.* **Neil Gibson**

Right Above: *A Hunterston to Drax Power Station loaded coal train with Class 66/0 No. 66078 in charge passes through Ribblehead station on 2 February 2007. In the background the iconic Ribblehead viaduct can be seen. When passenger services ceased the 'up' platform was removed and a siding into the quarry land which can be seen on the far left. When passenger services resumed a new platform was built in a staggered formation because of the quarry line.* **Richard Armstrong**

Right Below: *Class 66/0 No. 66149 passes Birkett Common with the Burngullow to Irvine loaded china clay 'silver bullet' train on 19 May 2007.* **Richard Armstrong**

West Midlands Metro – Phase 1

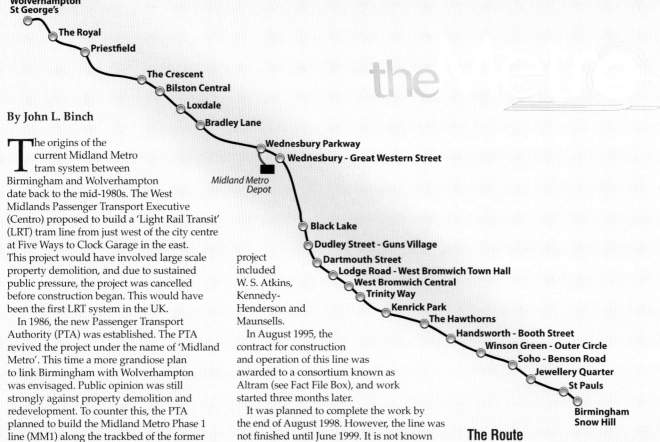

Wolverhampton St George's
The Royal
Priestfield
The Crescent
Bilston Central
Loxdale
Bradley Lane
Wednesbury Parkway
Wednesbury - Great Western Street
Midland Metro Depot
Black Lake
Dudley Street - Guns Village
Dartmouth Street
Lodge Road - West Bromwich Town Hall
West Bromwich Central
Trinity Way
Kenrick Park
The Hawthorns
Handsworth - Booth Street
Winson Green - Outer Circle
Soho - Benson Road
Jewellery Quarter
St Pauls
Birmingham Snow Hill

By John L. Binch

The origins of the current Midland Metro tram system between Birmingham and Wolverhampton date back to the mid-1980s. The West Midlands Passenger Transport Executive (Centro) proposed to build a 'Light Rail Transit' (LRT) tram line from just west of the city centre at Five Ways to Clock Garage in the east. This project would have involved large scale property demolition, and due to sustained public pressure, the project was cancelled before construction began. This would have been the first LRT system in the UK.

In 1986, the new Passenger Transport Authority (PTA) was established. The PTA revived the project under the name of 'Midland Metro'. This time a more grandiose plan to link Birmingham with Wolverhampton was envisaged. Public opinion was still strongly against property demolition and redevelopment. To counter this, the PTA planned to build the Midland Metro Phase 1 line (MM1) along the trackbed of the former Great Western Railway (GWR) Birmingham Snow Hill to Wolverhampton Low Level line (closed in 1972) for much of its length.

The Act of Parliament for the MM1 received Royal Assent in November 1989, and in April 1990, a funding application under Section 56 of the Transport Act (1968) was submitted, with £1.5 million being subsequently awarded. In March 1992, a further £3 million was granted by central government, thus increasing the total funding to £4.5 million. Consultants for the project included W. S. Atkins, Kennedy-Henderson and Maunsells.

In August 1995, the contract for construction and operation of this line was awarded to a consortium known as Altram (see Fact File Box), and work started three months later.

It was planned to complete the work by the end of August 1998. However, the line was not finished until June 1999. It is not known whether any compensation payments were made by Altram.

The construction cost of MM1 has never been disclosed. The prominent supporter of the Midland Metro, David Gilroy Bevan, told Parliament in 1990 that it would cost £60 million. Centro has since said that the line cost £145 million (1995 prices). However, this sum does not reflect various items such as a wheel lathe, that were deleted to reduce the headline sum.

The Route

The 12½ mile (20.2 km) line opened on 31 May 1999. The terminus at its Southern end is Birmingham Snow Hill station near St. Philip's Cathedral in the city centre. The line then runs parallel to the Network Rail (NR) line as far as The Hawthorns, where the tracks diverge. Trams continue along the route of the GWR line to Wolverhampton via West Bromwich, Wednesbury and Bilston, while the NR line veers to the left towards Smethwick Galton Bridge and beyond.

Above: On the afternoon of 18 January 2010, Midland Metro services were terminated at Soho Benson Road due to overhead line failure in the Jewellery Quarter area. Passengers for Birmingham Snow Hill used London Midland train services to and from The Hawthorns. Ansaldo T69 tram No. 04 stands at the ersatz terminus on the up 'wrong line' with the 15.25 service to Wolverhampton St. Georges. The tram crossed over onto the down line before the next stop at Winson Green Outer Circle. John Binch

The route continues along the former railway line as far as Priestfield where it swings to the left for its last leg along public roads to its Northern terminus at Wolverhampton St. George's in the city centre.

St. George's is near to Pipers Row bus station and around a 15 minute walk from the railway station. A Midland Metro maintenance depot was built on former railway sidings, alongside the Wednesbury Great Western Street tram stop.

Fact File
Altram and the Aftermath

When MM1 opened, Altram was a profit-making company owned by Ansaldo, Laing and Travel West Midlands (TWM). Upon opening, it soon became apparent to the three partners that the Midland Metro operating revenues would not be able to cover costs.

In 2001, Ansaldo announced that it was "not prepared to invest further monies in a loss-making venture which showed no prospect of ever becoming profitable". Laing then followed suit saying that the company "felt there was no economic future in Altram, and that to contribute further funds would only increase its loss in what it believed to be a failing project". In February 2003, the Midland Metro's auditors refused to sign off its accounts.

Ansaldo and Laing finally got out of the company. Day-to-day operation of the Midland Metro is now in the hands of Travel Midland Metro (TMM), which is now part of the National Express Group (NEG). Its losses are chiefly covered by cross subsidies received from other parts of the NE business.

The NEG is responsible for Midland Metro losses until 2019, although Centro plans to re-franchise the operation well before then, as part of the MM1 expansion programme. This would mean that the responsibility for any future losses would be transferred from NEG to the public sector.

The Trams

Sixteen type T69 trams, numbered 01 to 16, were built by Ansaldobreda, S.P.A., near Naples, in Italy. They are of a six-axle articulated two-section design operating from a 650V dc overhead power system.

Three entrances on each side are provided, and wheelchair access is in the centre portion only. The carriage of bicycles is not permitted. Due to accessibility limitations they are exempt from the Rail Vehicle Accessibility Regulations (1998).

When built, the trams were painted in the Midland Metro dark blue and light grey with green livery complete with yellow passenger doors and red front ends. Four trams, (Nos. 05, 07, 09, and 10) have since received the Travel West Midlands silver and pink colours following refurbishment.

Twelve trams have been named after local dignitaries and famous people from the West Midlands that are associated with the MM1 route (see Information Box 2).

Centro has stated that it would like to see the type T69 vehicles replaced. The Government has pledged support for a fleet of up to 25 new, longer trams which would increase the frequency of services to every six minutes throughout the day. The Metro would then carry 40 per cent more passengers during peak times and 75 per cent more people during the off peak. The project is hoped to commence before 2014. Therefore, new trams would be working within around fifteen years. This

Above: Loxdale in the Bilston suburbs was once in the hub of the extensive Black Country steel industry and is adjacent to the Sankey Engineering factory, which until the 1980s was the largest employer in the area. On the afternoon of 27 January 2010, tram Nos. 06 Alan Garner *(left) and 09* Jeff Astle *make for an interesting livery comparison as they make their brief stops. John Binch*

makes an interesting comparison with trams on other systems, such as the Manchester Metrolink, which have a 30 to 50 years lifespan.

The Service

Currently (early 2010*), trams run at an 8-minute frequency during the day from Monday to Saturday and at a 15-minute frequency on Sundays. The first tram departs from both Birmingham Snow Hill and Wolverhampton at 0515 (Monday to Saturday) and at 0800 on Sunday. The last trams depart both termini at 2330 (Monday to Saturday) and 2300 on Sunday. Earlier and later departures are available to both Birmingham and Wolverhampton from Wednesbury Parkway. The journey time is 35 minutes. Although this does not compare favourably with the rail service, it has the advantage of serving the centre of Wolverhampton and provides important commuter connections to non-rail served places such as Bilston, Handsworth,

Fact File
T69 Technical Data

Built	1998-99
Traction Motors	Four
Dimensions	24m x 2.65m
Doors	Sliding plug
Wheel arrangement	Bo – 2 – Bo
Braking	Rheostatic, regenerative, disc and magnetic track
Couplers	Not equipped
Weight	35.6t
Maximum speed	43mph (70kph)
Acceleration	0-50kph in 10seconds
Stopping distance from maximum speed	182m*
Seating capacity	56 (including 2 wheel chairs)
Maximum capacity	208

* in normal service conditions

Below: Wednesbury Great Western Street and Wednesbury Parkway are the closest two adjacent stations on the Midland Metro. On 2 February 2010, No. 14 Jim Eames *arrives at Wednesbury Parkway with a service for Wolverhampton St. Georges. Wednesbury Great Western Street can just be seen in the distance and the maintenance depot is on the right behind the tram. John Binch*

Above: *2009 marked the tenth anniversary of the opening of the Midland Metro Light Rail Transit system between Birmingham and Wolverhampton. On 1 October 2009, Ansaldo Transporti Type T69 Bo – 2 – Bo tram No. 07 Billy Wright in the latest pink and silver livery pauses at Bilston Central with an afternoon Wolverhampton St. Georges to Birmingham Snow Hill service. It is now difficult to believe that this cutting once reverberated to the sight and sound of GWR 'Castle' and 'King' class steam locomotives hauling crack express trains from London Paddington to Wolverhampton (Low Level)!* **John Binch**

and West Bromwich town centre. It was originally planned that the service would run at a 6-minute frequency, but this has never materialised.

A single adult ticket from Birmingham Snow Hill to Wolverhampton St. Georges costs £2.70, with a day return at £4.50 (January 2010*). A single ticket on a Travel West Midlands bus is £1.70 (2009 prices frozen in 2010). It has not been possible to keep the price of Midland Metro tickets broadly comparable to the price of bus tickets as was originally hoped, much to the chagrin of regular commuters!

When the service first started, tickets were purchased from machines located at each station. However, due to the increasing problem of vandalism and loss of revenue caused by fare evasion, tickets are now purchased from the on board conductor (or Customer Service Representatives as they are officially called!)

To run the intensive service there are 116 operations staff, 30 engineering staff, and 48 drivers.

Further Expansion Plans (Phase 1)

The patronage of the Midland Metro has been far lower than was envisaged (currently 14,000 passengers per day). The Midland Metro accounts for less than 2 per cent of journeys made by public transport in the West Midlands and no quantifiable relief of the adjacent A41 Birmingham to Wolverhampton road has been reported, suggesting that many commuters have failed to be persuaded to leave their cars at home and use the tram. However, despite this disappointing trend, expansion of the

Fact File – The Name Game

Tram	Name	Details
01	Sir Frank Whittle	Born 1 June 1907 in Coventry. Co-inventor of the jet engine, and hailed as the 'father of jet propulsion'. Died 9 September 1996.
03	Ray Lewis	Former Director of Technical Services for Wolverhampton City Council and involved in the development of the Midland Metro.
05	Sister Dora	Born 16 January 1832 as Dorothy Wyndlow Pattison. Became famous as a tireless and compassionate nurse, particularly to railwaymen, at Walsall's first hospital. Died 24 December 1878.
06	Alan Garner	Born 5 June 1929. Wolverhampton Labour councillor and former Vice-Chairman of the West Midlands Passenger Transport Executive (Centro). Died 1996.
07	Billy Wright	Born 6 February 1924. Football hero who spent his entire career at Wolverhampton Wanderers. He had 105 England caps, and was the first footballer in the world to attain 100 caps. He captained England for a record 90 times. Died 3 September 1994.
08	Joseph Chamberlain	Born 8 July 1836. Influential businessman, politician and statesman. Co-founded the Birmingham Education League and became Mayor of Birmingham in November 1873. MP for Birmingham in 1876. Died 2 July 1914.
09	Jeff Astle	Born 13 May 1909. West Bromwich Albion football legend known as 'The King' making 361 appearances and scoring 174 goals for the club. Also had five England caps. Died 19 January 2002.
10	John Stanley Webb	Walsall-born tram expert and author.
11	Theresa Stewart	Birmingham City Labour councillor who was Lord Mayor from May 2001 to May 2002.
13	Anthony Nolan	Born 1971. Suffered from the rare inherited Wiskott Aldrich Syndrome. Died 1979. Anthony's mother Shirley (1942-2002) set up the Anthony Nolan Trust in 1974, which has since helped over 5,800 children and adults with leukaemia.
14	Jim Eames	Former long-serving Birmingham City councillor and former Lord Mayor (1974).
15	Agenoria	Pioneer 0-4-0 steam locomotive built by John Urpeth Rastrick at Stourbridge in 1829. Named after the goddess of courage and industry. The oldest surviving locomotive from the Black Country. Now at the National Railway Museum, York.
16	Gerwyn John	A prominent engineer on the Midland Metro project.

Above: In March 2009, Centro proposed a new £60million Midland Metro Birmingham City Centre Extension (BCCE) line, terminating at Stephenson Street adjacent to New Street station. This is a much shortened version of the original BCCE route which was planned to go to Five Ways Shopping Centre via Broad Street at a cost of £180million. On the evening of 22 October 2009, Ansaldo T-69 tram No. 10 *John Stanley Webb* stands at the current Snow Hill terminus with the 20.14 service to Wolverhampton St. Georges. **John Binch**

system remains a top priority. Councillor Gary Clarke, chairman of Centro, said in 2006 that the Midland Metro would, "make a real impact on our campaign to cut congestion for everyone".

Centro has asked for Government money for two Phase 1 expansion plans:
Line 1: A 2.8km line from the current Birmingham Snow Hill station to Five Ways via New Street station and Broad Street known as the Birmingham City Centre Extension (BCCE). In 2005, an order authorising the City Centre Extension was made.
Line 2: An 11km line branching off from the current Metro line at Wednesbury, running to Brierley Hill via Dudley and the Merry Hill Shopping Centre along the trackbed of the disused Bescot to Stourbridge freight line.

Line 1: Birmingham City Centre Extension (BCCE), publicly, Centro favour this route which will bring a street tramway to the city centre of Birmingham for the first time since 1953. The route would leave the current Snow

Hill terminus and make its way down Bull Street and Corporation Street to New Street. Here the line would then make its way to Edgbaston Shopping Centre at Five Ways. At certain points, such as Suffolk Queensway the line would pass above street level on a bridge. The response of Birmingham City Council to this route has been inconsistent. Before 2005, it favoured running the line through a tunnel in the city centre but this idea has now been scrapped. The exact route has still to be confirmed.

The BCCE line would improve passenger access to the city centre particularly around Corporation Street and the Palisades Shopping Centre, but would severely impede bus access in the area. Also, up to 10 shops would have to be relocated.

The proposed re-routing of bus services has long been a bone of contention between Centro and National Express West Midlands (NXWM). In response, NXWM had attempted to divert busses to a new 'bus mall' at Moor Street

railway station. However, following several accidents, the mall was forced to close before it had fully opened. Therefore, the question of bus access along the BCCE route needs to be resolved before any work can begin.
The other major stumbling block has been obtaining funding for the project. In 2005, it was estimated that BCCCE line would cost £72million; however, a 2008 report put the figure at £180million! Perhaps the coup de grace of this ambitious scheme came in 2007 when Centro refused to fund the associated traffic congestion charge scheme along Broad Street. Because of this and the escalating costs, an alternative shorter line was drawn up in March 2009 which would terminate at Stephenson Street and provide a direct connection with New Street railway station. This line is estimated to cost a mere £60million.

Line 2: The Brierley Hill Extension - This route is planned to leave the current Line 1 at Wednesbury and then use the trackbed of the abandoned South Staffordshire Railway, to

Right: *One major town to be served by the Metro is West Bromwich. The main stop in the town centre is West Bromwich Central which is conveniently situated adjacent to the bus station and provides an excellent public transport interchange. On 18 January 2010, tram No. 10* John Stanley Webb *makes its stop with a Birmingham Snow Hill bound service. The Metro is certainly the better way to travel to the city centre of Birmingham; with a journey time of just 13 minutes compared to the Travel West Midlands No. 74 or 79 bus which often takes over 30 minutes.* **John Binch**

Above: *From 30 August to 28 September 2008 no Midland Metro services operated into the Wolverhampton St. Georges tram stop. This was to allow the painting of Wishbone Bridge which is located where the tracks cross the Wolverhampton Ring Road near the city centre. Between 30 August and 2 September services terminated at the Priestfield tram stop, and from 3 September onwards services were extended to The Royal tram stop. Metro services operated normally between Priestfield / The Royal and Birmingham Snow Hill tram stops. Photographed in poor light on 31 August 2008, tram No. 09* **Jeff Astle** *negotiates the little used Priestfield cross-over onto the up line ready to form the 15.50 service to Birmingham Snow Hill.* **John Binch**

Sandwell and then on to the former Dudley Town station. Here the line would run at street level into Dudley town centre, before leaving the town alongside the southern bypass road to regain the railway trackbed.

The line would diverge again on the approach to the Waterfront/Merry Hill shopping area and Brierley Hill. At one point services were due to start in 2011, though this is now unlikely to happen.

Centro hope to run ten trams per hour along the route serving both Birmingham and Wolverhampton alternatively. A journey time of 31 minutes from Brierley Hill to West Bromwich is envisaged.

In 2000 the cost of the line was estimated to be £114.1million (1999 prices). By 2005 this had risen to £139million and incredibly this figure had almost doubled to £268million the following year! Therefore, as in the situation regarding the BCCE route, the problem of funding the escalating costs need to be resolved before any work can begin.

On a positive note some preliminary work has been carried out. In 2005 - 06, the 50 year old Tipton Road over bridge in Dudley was rebuilt. Centro Director General, Geoff Inskip has proposed spending almost £2million to purchase land for a car park at Dudley Port. A further £10 million would be required for the compulsory purchase of land required for the Brierley Hill extension.

In 2008, Centro came up with the 'Wednesbury – Brierley Hill – Stourbridge Rapid Transit' plan. This involves converting the Brierley Hill Extension into an integrated passenger and freight 'tram-train' line linking Wednesbury with Stourbridge, via the re-

opening of the South Staffordshire railway from Bescot. Centro said that, "running freight trains on the proposed tram tracks will remove the need to build a separate track for freight alongside the Metro rails, cutting overall construction costs by around 20 per cent". However, no evidence of the need for the line, or any cost saving, has been given. In fact, during construction of Line 1, a flyover was built at great expense at Handsworth ensuring that the tram lines were totally separate to freight trains serving the scrap metal terminal. If the track sharing plan came into operation, trams on the route would cross the path of freight trains ten times, on each return journey to Stourbridge. Therefore, it is difficult to see how this scheme would work in practice, especially if there is an upturn in freight (or passenger) traffic along the route.

Although this scheme is still very much in its infancy, detailed studies into this track sharing concept have continued into 2010 when an Outline Business Case seeking government money was being prepared by Centro.

Further Expansion Plans (Phase 2)

Birmingham City Centre to Great Barr - this 10km, route with 17-stops would run from the City Centre through Lancaster Circus and along the A34 corridor to a Park and Ride interchange with the M6 Junction 7 at Great Barr. The route designated 'Varsity North' by Centro has been branded 'a white elephant' by Khalid Mahmood, the MP for Birmingham Perry Bar. Nonetheless, Centro issued a pre-planning notice in late 2009 to investigate ways of developing a business plan for the project.

A Transport and Works Act Order is already in place, but funding has yet to be secured.

Negotiations have started with Network Rail and local authorities to look into a track sharing scheme between trams and trains. The project is at a very early stage and work is not due start until 2012. Completion is envisaged for 2018, and is estimated to cost some £432million.

Possible Other Routes

■ Birmingham City Centre to Quinton - a line running for 7.5km from the Birmingham City Centre Extension (BCCE) terminus at Five Ways which would continue along the Hagley Road to Quinton. This plan relies on the completion of the BCCE line to Five Ways.

■ Birmingham City Centre to Birmingham International Airport - this 14km route would link Birmingham City Centre at Bull Street with the Birmingham International Airport/NEC complex as well as serving the conurbation along the main A45 Coventry road.

The proposed terminus will be sited about 600 metres away from the airport, and will be nearer to Birmingham International. Although a journey time of 29 minutes is envisaged to the Airport check-in, this is comparable to existing bus services, and not competitive with the rail service; as Birmingham International is only 10 minutes away by train from Birmingham New Street station in the city centre.

■ Wolverhampton City Centre to Wednesfield, Willenhall, Walsall and Wednesbury - designated the '5Ws' by Centro, this 20.4km line, would link Wolverhampton City Centre with Wednesfield, Willenhall, Walsall and Wednesbury, and provide access to both

Above: *Tram No. 06 Alan Garner arrives at Lodge Road West Bromwich Town Hall on 20 February 2010 with a Birmingham Snow Hill service. Services were only running as far as Priestfield on this day due to traffic light failure in Wolverhampton city centre. Passengers at this stop would suffer further inconvenience as the lift was also out of order!* **John Binch**

New Cross and Manor Hospitals. The route would partially use the trackbed of the former Wolverhampton and Walsall Railway.
■ Wolverhampton City Centre Loop - this route estimated to cost £30 million would be an extension to the existing Phase 1 route designed to serve both bus and railway stations in Wolverhampton.

The Current Situation
In its 2009 draft Integrated Public Transport Prospectus, Centro has claimed that light rail typically costs between £10-20 million per kilometre. This does not agree with estimates for the Phase One extensions of £64.28 million/km for the Birmingham City Centre Extension, and £24.36 million/km for the Brierley Hill Extension Route).

A director was due to be appointed to investigate ways of raising the additional funds required. However, in January 2009, this £100k per annum post was scrapped.

The Wolverhampton city centre loop has since gained preference over the Brierley Hill route and pending successful business case applications the Department for Transport has agreed to pay £53 million towards the project.

In July 2009, it appeared that plans for the New Street to Five Ways section of the Birmingham City Centre Extension had stalled. However, following a discussion with MPs and the Transport Minister Chris Cole in January 2010, Centro Chief Executive Geoff Inskip has urged ministers to make a quick decision about the route.

On 18 March 2010, the DfT finally granted Program Entry Status (initial approval) for an extension as far as New Street station. The extension now costing some £127.1million will run approximately 1km along Bull Street and Corporation Street and terminate at Stephenson Street (adjacent to New Street station).

Trams will no longer use Snow Hill station itself but will be diverted over a £9milion

viaduct. This will provide an important city centre public transport interchange as part of New Street station's £600million redevelopment.

Also included are a fleet on 19 new trams which are larger and more suited to on-street running than the current vehicles, which will be replaced. The new vehicles will have a capacity of 200 passengers. Existing stops along the route will be extended to accommodate the new trams, and a new depot will be built at Wednesbury.

The new project which is expected to generate 3.5million passengers annually is partly funded via the Regional Funding Allocation process with the DfT providing up to £81million. Centro hopes that the extension will boost the regional economy by £50million and generate 1,300 new jobs. Despite the fact that the extension through to Five Ways is now unlikely to happen, the New Street extension will improve access to Birmingham city centre and according to TramForward it will "tackle the city's chronic congestion problems."

Signalling
Tram movements are controlled by the black disc/white dot matrix system with five lamps being lit for each aspect. Along the streets of Wolverhampton, tram signals are integrated with traffic lights. Trams are driven on sight, with proceed indicators (vertical line) permit a driver to pass if the road is clear of obstruction.

Accidents
Since the line opened, several trams have collided with road vehicles either at crossings, or on the street section through Wolverhampton. Also, there has been more than one collision reported between two trams.

As well as electrical and mechanical failure of the tram system, vandalism has led to many disruptions. In the summer of 2001, the section through the streets of Wolverhampton was

closed for a time due to an electrocution risk.

Interestingly, criminal activity was not successfully dealt with at the planning stage and the high crime rate led to the installation of closed circuit television inside trams and the removal of the tram stop ticket machines.

The responsibility to investigate accidents on the Midland Metro currently lies with the Rail Accident Investigation Board.

Metro Pub Crawl
In 2007, Travel West Midlands introduced the Metro Good Pubs Guide leaflet giving details of pubs within a short distance of Midland Metro stops. 23 pubs are included ranging from J D Wetherspoons free houses to specialist real ale venues.

The author's favourite is The Wellington on Bennetts Hill a short walk from Snow Hill station. This pub serves over 2,500 real ales annually and is the 2009 Birmingham CAMRA Pub of the Year.

The Black Eagle in Hockley (Soho Benson Road stop) and the Olde White Rose in Bilston (Bilston Central stop) with their wide choice of real ale and excellent food are also recommended.

A pub guide is also available via the Midland Metro home page.

Links
Further information can be obtained from the following web sites:
● Midland Metro:
    www.midlandmetro.co.uk
● Centro Midland Metro:
    www.centro.org.uk/Metro
● Light Rail Transit Association:
    www.lrta.org
● Rail Around Birmingham and the West Midlands-Midland Metro:
    www.railaroundbirmingham.
    co.uk/midland_metro.php

The Canadian Turbotrain

By Keith Ewins

In the mid to late 1960s passenger train travel in the USA appeared to be in terminal decline and few companies were interested in operating passenger services. In Canada at this time the Government took a more enlightened view, and had tried hard to retain what it considered to be important public transport. Canadian National, then State owned, continued to advertise and support passenger trains although it must be said that privately owned Canadian Pacific was less inclined, but maintained well what it was forced to keep operating with grant aid.

The major corridor of Montréal–Toronto was and still is seen as worthy of passenger development. With this in mind, it was decided in 1967 to invest in a futuristic gas turbine train for service on this route. The trains were built to operate alongside existing trains such as the locomotive hauled 'Rapidos' (premier conventional trains) and were expected to save 49 minutes on the regular scheduled services.

The Turbo had been conceived by United Aircraft Corporation (UAC) of Farmington, Connecticut, USA, in conjunction with United Aircraft of Canada Ltd, Pratt & Whitney Canada (UACL/PWC) of Longueil, Quebec, and built for the American Department of Transport (DOT) as a prototype light weight passenger train which saw experimental public service between New York and Boston. Also for Canadian National for service between Toronto and Montréal.

The Canadian Turbos used ST6 gas turbine engines designed and built by United Aircraft of Canada Ltd in its Longueil, Quebec plant and were a modified Pratt & Whitney Aircraft PT6 turbine used in turbo-prop aircraft, helicopters, marine and industrial applications.

The train itself was designed by Sikorsky Aircraft, Connecticut, USA, a division of UAC. The Canadian trains were built by MLW Worthington, formerly Montréal Locomotive Works Ltd, and later Bombardier Canada under contract to United Aircraft of Canada and delivered to them for testing before delivery to Canadian National on a lease maintenance basis.

The agreement gave CN the option for outright purchase. Five seven-car trains were ordered and could operate in multiple if required. In 1973 they were reformed into three nine-car sets, surplus cars going to form new five-car sets for use in the United States, operating alongside American constructed

Above: Formed of set No. CN3, led by driving power car No. 129, with No. 154 bringing up the rear, train No. 67, the 16.30 Montréal to Toronto passes Brockville First Avenue (Mp124.1) at 18.10 on 18 August 1975. Don McQueen

Left: An aluminium driving car for a CN Turbo set is seen under assembly in the main erecting hall at Montreal Locomotive Works. The view illustrates the construction using strong aluminium alloy resistant to normal ambient temperature, most joints were welded giving a very strong structure. CN

Above: *The 07.45 Toronto to Montréal 'Turbo' on 10 July 1975 is seen arriving in Kingston, with the Cataraqui River in the background. The train is formed of set No. CN2, with driving power car No. 125 (of type PDC-26), power car No. 150 brings up the rear of the train.* **Don McQueen**

Below: *The first of the Canadian National 'Turbo' sets No. CN1, with power car No. P100 poses outside the shed at Montreal Locomotive Works in the autumn of 1968.* **CN**

Souvenir ticket of your trip on

turbo

commemorating the return of today's most exciting way to travel between Toronto and Montreal, June 22, 1973.

CN

Above: *In the original seven-car formation, a pre-service working of a Turbo is seen on the outskirts of Toronto in January 1969. The leading driving car is No. P202, which was later renumbered to 152.* Bryce Lee

Left: *A seven car CN-liveried Turbo set, led by driving car No. P204 is seen at Dorval near Montréal in the early 1970s before being reformed into a nine-car set.* J. D. Welch

Below: *Nine-car set No. CN1, led by driving car No 125, a PDC-27 vehicle set out for Turbolux (second class) seating. The train is seen arriving at Toronto Union station in April 1974 as empty stock from Spadina coach yard prior to forming train No. 66 to Montréal. This part of Toronto Union station is now used for the expanding GO Transit services.* Bryce Lee

Above: With its sliding plug doors open and the retractable steps in the lowered position, a nine-car 'Turbo' set is seen at the new Ottawa Union Station on 19 August 1975. The train is No. 36, the afternoon Ottawa to Montréal service. The Ottawa service was formed of the spare 'Turbo' set which would have otherwise stood in the sidings not earning revenue, and operated to standard locomotive hauled schedules. The train is led by driving car No. 129, with No. 154 on the rear the intermediate vehicles are No. 204, 263, 259, 226, 264, 254, 257. Don McQueen

turbos built by Pullman Standard in 1967 for the New York to Boston route.

Technically the CN Turbos were ahead of their time and carried many unique innovations over conventional trains. A single unit contained four gas turbine engines, two in each domed car with an additional turbine in one dome car to supply electrical power for heating and air conditioning. As with the British High Speed Train (HST) both power cars were under power and could be driven from either end in the leading cab.

The engines powered the train through a mechanical drive and burnt conventional No. 2 (red) diesel fuel. In power comparisons (engines only) the turbines weighed less than one pound per horsepower produced, whereas a typical diesel (engine only) at that time required about 15 pounds to produce one horsepower of traction. The turbines engines weighed about

Below: A pre-production mock-up of a Turbo driving car type PDC-26, a first class vehicle, showing the single swivel first class seating in the upper lounge area. The cut-out below, shows the position of the ST6 gas-turbine Turbo engines. CN

300 pounds and produced 400 hp for traction purposes.

Diesel engine warm ups and pre-operational idling are not required for turbines and they could be started quickly at temperatures down to 60° F below zero and reach full power within half a minute, thus saving fuel and requiring less maintenance.

The engines used, identified as ST6 were some of the quietest gas turbines ever built. By North American standards the train was light weight, this was achieved by using aluminium for construction of the body and

some of the key components. Bogies were only used on the powered dome driving cars, all trailing cars were mounted on single axles. The transmission was a light-weight geared arrangement which drove the axles through drive shafts. Weight was not the only concern in the design, although it was an important factor in contributing to train resistance. Aerodynamic drag at speeds above 80 mph had to be accounted for and therefore the train was streamlined throughout. The fibreglass nose was bulbous, the roof, sides and belly of the Turbos were curved, the aluminium skin was

Fact File
Turbo Train formations 1967 – 1972

Vehicle Type	Set CN1	Set CN2	Set CN3	Set CN4	Set CN5
PDC-26	125 (P100)	126 (P101)	127 (P102)	128 (P103)	129 (P104)
IC-33	200 (T100)	201 (T101)	202 (T102)	203 (T103)	204 (T104)
IC-35	255 (T202)	256 (T205)	257 (T208)	258 (T211)	259 (T214)
IC-34	260 (T201)	261 (T204)	262 (T207)	263 (T210)	264 (T213)
IC-31	225 (T300)	226 (T301)	227 (T302)	228 (T303)	229 (T304)
IC-30	250 (T200)	251 (T203)	252 (T206)	253 (T209)	254 (T212)
PDC-27	150 (P200)	151 (P201)	152 (P202)	153 (P203)	154 (P204)

Above: A nine-car 'Turbo' set led by power car No. 126 with No. 151 on the rear is seen near Brockville, while forming train 63 from Toronto to Montréal, making a meet with CN5555 a GP38-2. Note the cross-bucks for the private grade crossing, which inhibited the full potential of these trains in terms of speed. Don McQueen

Left: Painted in the later VIA yellow livery, a standard nine-car 'Turbo' with car No. 154 nearest the camera is seen at Kingston on 11 August 1980 with train 66, the 15.50 Toronto Montréal. Don McQueen

Below: With nearly as much vegetation between the rails as on the track side, a VIA 'Turbo' set led by car No. 151 with No. 146 trailing, passes Kingston Mills near Kingston, with train No. 65 from Montréal to Toronto on 15 July 1982. Don McQueen

smooth and the doors and tinted glass windows fitted flush. The overall profile or cross section of the train was smaller than conventional equipment although the floor area of the saloons was wider.

The single axles on the trailer cars were also unique in that they were guided, that is the Turbo was actually steered around curves and did not depend entirely on the wheel flange contact. Added to this was the innovative suspension system which supported the cars from above, providing a pendular action which made the body bank inward on curves (tilting). This system together with a centre of gravity only 40 inches off the rails provided comfort whilst allowing higher speeds on existing track especially on curves which would have inhibited conventional trains.

North American railways demand very strict safety requirements in any build of passenger equipment and although light weight, Turbo still had to conform to all the standards of the Association of American Railroads (AAR) for strength and rigidity. This was achieved by constructing the frames and body members from a strong aluminium alloy resistant to corrosion and not affected by normal ambient temperature. Most joints were welded, a process which made joints as strong as the metal sections themselves.

The design and specification of these trains allowed them to negotiate curves at much higher speeds than the conventional 'Rapido' service which ran the 335 mile route between Montréal and Toronto at an average speed of

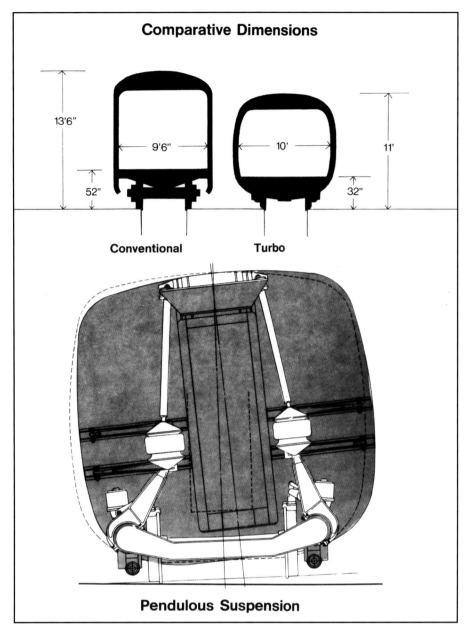

Comparative Dimensions

13'6"   9'6"   10'   11'

52"   32"

Conventional   Turbo

Pendulous Suspension

Below: *After some Ontario snow, train No. 60, the 08.00 Toronto to Montréal is photographed slowing for its Kingston stop at 09.35 on 27 December 1978. The train is formed of set No. CN3, led by driving car No. 129 which shows signs of serious impact damage to one of the fibreglass front doors.* **Don McQueen**

Fact File
Turbo Train formations 1973 – 1982

Vehicle Type	Set CN1	Set CN2	Set CN3
PDC-26	125 (145¤)	126 (146¤)	129 (149¤)
IC-33	200	201	204
IC-33	202	203	263[1]
IC-35	255	256	259
IC-31	225	226	229
IC-34	260	261	264
IC-30	250	251	254
IC-31	227	228	257[2]
PDC-27	150 / 153[3]	151	154

¤ Renumbered to the VIA 14x series in 1979
[1] Rebuilt from an IC-34 vehicle
[2] Rebuilt from an IC-35 vehicle
[3] 150 was replaced by 153 in 1976

Above: Showing the early VIA/CN yellow livery carried pre-1978, driving car No. 153 leads a 'Turbo' set away from Toronto Union on 25 April 1976. The train is the 08.00 service bound for Montréal, train No. 61. The building behind the leading car is the Okeefe Centre for Performing Arts. Don McQueen Collection

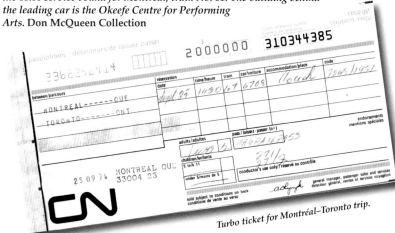

Turbo ticket for Montréal–Toronto trip.

Montréal/Ottawa–Toronto timetable April-October 1974.

MONTRÉAL — TORONTO OTTAWA — TORONTO

♈ ☆ Cavalier 59 Daily Quot.	② ☆ ④ The Exec. L'. Exec.. 45 Daily Quot.	Bona- venture 55 Daily Quot.	① ★ ③ Turbo 67 Daily Quot.	★ Rapido 61 Daily Quot.	Lake- shore 51 Daily Quot.	① tarian 647 Ex. Sun. Sauf dim.	Miles Milles	24 Eastern Time Heure de l'Est	Lake- shore 50 Daily Quot.	★ Rapido 60 Daily Quot.	① ★ ③ Turbo 66 Daily Quot.	☆ Bona- venture 54 Daily Quot.	② ☆ ④ The Exec. L'. Exec.. 44 Daily Quot.	① tarian 648 Ex. Sat. Sauf sam.	♈ ☆ Cavalier 58 Daily Quot.
23 30	. .	16 50	. .	11 30	09 00	. .	0.0 Dp	**Montréal, Qué.** Ar	15 24	16 29	20 40	22 20	. .	. .	07 30
23 55	. .	17 13	16 47	11 52	09 22	. .	11.5	Dorval ▲ . ①. .	14 55	16 04	20 14	21 55	. .	. .	07 05
00 58	. .	18 03	. .	. .	10 15	. .	69.2	Cornwall, Ont. . .	14 03	. .	. .	21 00	. .	. .	06 00
. .	. .	. .	. .	. .	10 52	. .	115.0	Prescott . ①. .	13 24	. .	. .	. .	. .	. .	. .
②④ ▼ **49** Ex. Sat. Sauf sam.		**Daily** **41** Quot.					**40** ①④ Daily Quot.						**48** ②④ ▼ Ex. Sat. Sauf sam.		
23 30	17 20	. .	. .	. .	09 10	. .	0.0 Dp	**Ottawa, Ont.** . Ar	15 15	. .	. .	22 45	. .	. .	†06 30
⊠00 50 ⋙	⊕ 18 25	. .	. .	. .	⊕ 10 15	. .	48.7	Smiths Falls ① .	⊕ 14 02	. .	. .	⊕ 21 32	. .	. .	⊠05 30 ◄
. .	19 15	. .	. .	. .	11 00	. .	76.2 Ar	Brockville . Dp	13 25	. .	. .	20 55	. .	. .	. .
02 25	19 20	18 54	. .	. .	11 12	. .	126.8 Dp	Brockville . Ar	13 09	. .	20 13	20 50	. .	. .	04 45
. .	. .	. .	. .	. .	11 38	. .	155.1	Gananoque . ①.	12 35	. .	. .	. .	. .	. .	■03 48
03 18	20 02	19 38	. .	. .	12 00	07 20	174.2	Kingston	12 15	. .	19 28	20 05	. .	22 09	03 23
. .	. .	. .	. .	. .	12 25	07 42	200.1	Napanee	11 47	. .	. .	. .	. .	21 46	①■02 46
04 50 ◄	20 50	20 25	. .	. .	12 55	08 07	221.9	Belleville	11 22	. .	18 44	19 20	. .	21 20	A01 50 ►
. .	. .	. .	. .	. .	. .	08 21	234.0	Trenton Jct . ①.	. .	. .	. .	. .	. .	21 06	■01 28
①05 45	21 25	21 05	. .	. .	13 35	08 45	265.2	Cobourg	10 44	. .	18 06	18 42	. .	20 38	①01 04
①06 00	. .	. .	. .	. .	. .	08 55	271.9	Port Hope . . .	. .	. .	. .	. .	. .	20 29	①00 50
①06 41	22 05	21 40	. .	. .	14 18	09 25	303.4	Oshawa . ①. .	10 05	. .	17 30	18 05	. .	20 02	①00 17
07 04	22 23	22 00	20 17	16 05	14 38	09 42	329.4	Guildwood ①△	09 46	11 50	16 47	17 11	17 48	19 47	23 53
07 30	22 45	22 20	20 40	16 29	14 59	09 59	335.0 Ar	**Toronto, Ont.** . Dp	09 25	11 30	16 30	16 50	17 30	19 30	23 30

Above: *Carrying the early VIA/CN yellow livery, a turbo hurries past the Toronto suburb of Scarborough, served by GO Transit. The train is heading into Toronto with train No. 61 which departed Montréal at 08.00 in May 1976.* Bryce Lee

67 mph. Turbo was diagrammed to travel at an average speed of 80 mph, saving 49 minutes. Its top speed was to be 95 mph (the design specification was 125 mph) in regular service, the same incidentally as conventional passenger equipment. The savings were achieved by the use of the tilt mechanism and the easing of restrictions on many of the curves.

The 1973 reformed Turbos operated as nine car sets, made up of two power cars with passenger domes and seven trailers which contained a café car, a club car (first class) and standard class cars known as 'Turbolux'. As with the structural and external design the interior was also radical and modern compared with the heavy streamlined cars of the 1950s which operated in the 'Rapidos'.

Seating was wide and reclined, the leading power car dome was club class and contained eight large revolving reclining chairs, the lower level had padded black leather upholstery seats with individual reading lights. 'Turboluxe' seats were similar using a blue material for upholstery with black leather headrest. The train was carpeted throughout, windows were curtained, all seats had individually controlled reading lights and fold down tables.

Luggage racks for carry-on baggage were located near the doors in the centre of each car.

Because there were no vestibules, passengers had uninterrupted views down the centre isle from car to car, providing a much improved interior ambiance.

Turbo drivers were located in the Dome driving cars, with their position on the right hand side in the direction of travel and separated from the passenger area by a glass partition, thus providing passengers with a view ahead.

The cars were slightly pressurised to keep out dirt, snow, heat and cold. They were electrically air conditioned in summer and electrically heated in winter. Doors were electrically operated and operated remotely from control stations located at each door. Entranceways had steps which could be aligned for stepping 'up' or 'down' depending on platform level.

Catering on board Turbo was provided by

a buffet equipped with microwave ovens and all the latest innovations. Club (first) class were served at seat, 'Turboluxe' passengers collected their food from the buffet counter.

Turbo club passengers were served their meals by smartly dressed hostesses whilst stewards served beverages. Beverages were also served in the rear 'Turboluxe' dome from a small bar to a drinks area provided with seats around small tables. Domes at first had full glass roofs as well as forward, rear and side glass. These roof areas had to be plated over due to the heat from the exhaust stacks melting the glass but excellent viewing was still achieved.

A small speedometer for passengers to observe train speed was provided in the domes.

As with any new and radical prototype there were problems, exhaust fires and mechanical design faults amongst them. These kept the trains from regular service for a number of years. When reformed from seven cars to nine cars in 1973 most of these problems had been ironed out and Canadian National relaunched the prestige service in April 1974 with one train each way between Toronto and Montréal, this increased to two each way in 1976 when a Kingston stop was inserted and connecting service to Ottawa was provided, previously the train only called at Guildwood in the Toronto suburbs and Dorval in the Montréal area close to Pierre Elliot Trudeau International Airport.

On 6 August 1974 the third unit was used to start a Montréal – Ottawa service. (as a spare unit it was rarely needed). The daily service replaced conventional train sets forming train Nos. 31 and 32 and it ran to a schedule 119 mins for the 116 miles westbound and 140 mins east bound due to extra stops at Alexandra and Coteau.

This Ottawa service was set up in direct competition to a new STOL (short take off and landing) air services using De Haviland 'Twin Otter' aircraft seating 11 passengers. It is interesting to note fares of various modes of transport at the time for this route. Conventional flights by Air Canada including transfer City centre to City centre took 100-120 mins, fare one way CN$18.00, STOL services took 75-80 mins

and cost CN$20.00 while the Turbo took 119 mins at a ticket price of CN$7.00.

Unfortunately disaster struck the Turbo operation on 23 September 1975 when fire broke out on an Ottawa service causing extensive damage to the first two cars, putting the entire train out of service for some considerable time. The Montréal – Ottawa service then reverted to using conventional equipment.

The Turbo set was repaired using cars from one of the trains reformed for Amtrak use, and partly destroyed in a collision at Lachine Quebec before delivery. Turbo, as a small fleet appeared to have had extreme bad luck with a number of cars including power cars lost during their lifetime but fortunately with no loss of life.

From 1976 the striking black, white and red livery gave way to the yellow and blue of the forthcoming VIA rail operation, a Crown operated company formed to take over all CN and CP main line passenger services from 1 April 1978. As part of this new look launch an invited passenger list including the press were taken from Kingston to Montréal on 22 April 1976 on a high speed extra service on which a Canadian rail speed record was achieved of 140.6 mph (226.3 km/h) which still stands to this day. In the period 1976 to 1978 CN and later VIA purchased the trains outright and took over the responsibility for maintenance previously provided by United Aircraft and CN.

A number of modifications were made at this time which rendered the trains to be far more efficient, even before this, the trains had an excellent reliability record. In the period 1973-1976 one million miles were covered with 98.6% availability albeit at some considerable cost in regular and strict maintenance regimes.

Alongside Turbos relative success Bombardier Canada was developing a new high speed rapid and comfortable train known as LRC (Light, Rapid and Comfortable). Test runs with a prototype locomotive and passenger cars were taking place as early as 1974 and a full train set was running by 1978. A decision had to be made as to the future needs for passenger services on Canada's passenger corridors in Ontario and Quebec.

Above: *With car No. 125 leading, set No. CN1 heads for Toronto Union through Scarborough in May 1976. The train would have previously called at the outer-suburban stop of Guildwood.* Bryce Lee

Pratt & Whitney had been prepared to build more Turbos for CN, the Crown Corporation wanted three but were told that a minimum order of five would be required to make the project viable. CN declined to order and LRC project won the day.

The Turbo trains had been and still were extremely popular with the travelling public, and when on one occasion the Kingston stop was taken out of the timetables there was a public outcry. The train quickly returned to the old schedule.

Services regularly loaded between 90% and 100% but that was not to save them,

the LRC was up and running with limited success between Montréal and Quebec by the early 1980s. CN was eager to put them on the premier route soon after, leaving just one Turbo return trip to cover for reliability problems of LRC.

The last Turbo run came on 31 October 1982. CN2 and CN3 were sent to Naporono Iron and Metal in Newark, New Jersey, USA in early 1983 for scrapping, the US Turbos were previously scrapped here in 1981 after the US lost interest in the project, again largely because the trains were none standard and Sikorsky had decided to pull out of train building.

Set CN1 which could have been a candidate for preservation if more interest had been shown, was scrapped in Lavel, Quebec in 1985, in hindsight a sad and remiss act.

As a postscript to Turbo it must be said that the power cars of its successor LRC were a failure and all had been withdrawn after only 10 years service. LRC cars today are hauled by conventional US designed passenger locomotives.

No one can say that Canada did not try to keep the passenger train high profile in the public's eye for in Turbo they operated one of the finest looking in the world. ∎

Below: *Looking very work stained, driving car No. 151 is seen at the Kingston stop on 11 August 1980, while forming Train No. 67, the 15.50 Montréal to Toronto Union. Note the fold out steps allowing easy access to the station platform, and the dirty patch on the front where the previously applied CN branding was attached.* Don McQueen

Fact File
US DoT formations
1968 – 1972

Vehicle Type	Set DoT 1	Set DoT 2
PDC-28	50	52
IC-29	70	71
PDC-29	51	53

Right: On 23 September 1975, set No. CN1 led by car No. 150 working a Montréal to Ottawa train caught fire on the approach to Coteau Quebec. The exhaust stack housing set fire to the carpets which quickly spread throughout the leading three vehicles. The set was subsequently withdrawn and later reformed with vehicles purchased back from the US train. After this event, services between Montréal to Ottawa reverted to loco-hauled 'Rapido' operation. Don McQueen Collection

Fact File
US Amtrak formations 1972 – 1976

Vehicle Type	Set Amtrak 1	Set Amtrak 2
PDC-28	50	52
IC-36	70	73
IC-29	71 (ex-70)	74 (ex-71)
IC-37	72	75
PDC-29	51	53

Vehicle Type	Set Amtrak 3[1]	Set Amtrak 3[2]
PDC-126	56 (ex-CN 127)	54 (ex-CN 128)
IC-131	70 (ex-CN 252)	77 (ex CN 253)
IC-134	78 (ex-CN 262)	76 (ex-CN 135, ex-CN 258)
PDC-127	57 (ex-CN152)	55 (ex CN 153)[3]

[1] New to Amtrak 3 October 1973
[2] Destroyed by fire 20 July 1973 on delivery to Amtrak
[3] Car 55 rebuilt following fire and later sold to CN and rebuilt as car CN 153 for set CN1

Left: The driving cab of end vehicle No. 129, showing the rotary power controller in front of the driving position.
Don McQueen

Right: The remains of driving car No. 150 (as No. 50) is seen mounted on Canadian National gondola car No. CN149324 in the London CN Reclamation Yard on 12 April 1981 awaiting breaking up. Don McQueen

Technical Data

Length - PDC	73ft 3in (22.33m)
Length - IC	56ft 10in (17.32m)
Height - over dome	12ft 11in (3.94m)
Height - over roof	10ft 11in (3.33m)
Width	10ft 5in (3.18m)
Train length (9-car)	544ft 4in (165.91m)
Floor height	31in (0.79m)
Wheel diam	30in (0.76m)
Passengers (9-car)	376 + 24 in lounge
Weight	220 tonnes
Speed (max)	125mph (201km/h)
Speed (service)	95mph (153km/h)
Power	4 x ST-6K of 600hp
Operating range	1200 mls (1931km)

The Highland Main Line

By Chris Perkins

The original Highland Main Line route between Perth and Inverness was via Forres but the opening of the Inverness and Aviemore Direct Railway in 1898 allowed a much shorter route of 118 miles from Stanley Junction seven miles north of Perth. Much of the line is single track with a few sections of double track and passing loops at some stations. There are some significant engineering works and gradients throughout the length of the line and the first of these features when travelling northwards from Perth is at Killiecrankie, where the line passes through a very narrow gorge and over a viaduct above the River Garry.

At Blair Atholl, a 23 mile section of double track commences which includes the climb to Druimuachdar summit. At 1,484 feet above sea level this is the highest point on the British rail system. The double line section finishes at Dalwhinnie where the highest whisky distillery in Scotland is located alongside the line. From here the line is single with passing loops for the next 52 miles.

Some 90 miles from Perth the line passes Aviemore which is a major holiday resort in both summer and winter. There is also a mainline connection with the Strathspey Railway, a preserved line which is regularly used by the Royal Scotsman VIP charter trains. From here, the line climbs to a summit at Slochd which is just over 1,300 feet above sea level, and then drops downgrade mostly

on gradients of 1:60 all the way to Inverness. Shortly after Slochd the line passes over the spectacular Findhorn viaduct at Tomatin high above the River Findhorn and five miles further on at Moy it crosses over a small river on the Alt-na-Slanach timber viaduct. This viaduct was constructed in 1887 and was the last remaining timber viaduct on a mainline in the UK and is a Grade A listed structure, but in recent years it had been suffering from severe fungal decay. This resulted in a speed reduction being imposed of 40 mph for passenger trains and 20 mph for freight trains. In 2003 the viaduct was strengthened with a new structure within the existing bridge which allowed the outside timbers to remain as built and look the same. The end of the single track section comes after it crosses the River Nairn on the 28 arch Culloden viaduct and Inverness is reached some eight miles further on.

Regular passenger services today are provided by First ScotRail and formed of Class 170 'Turbostars'. They run roughly every two hours between Perth and Inverness although not all services stop at all stations. There is also a nightly sleeper service between London Euston and Inverness which is Class 67 hauled north of Edinburgh. This service does not run southbound on a Saturday or northbound on a Sunday.

East Coast, formally National Express East Coast, have a daily HST service (except Sundays) between London King's Cross and

Inverness under the banner of the 'Highland Chieftain'. The northbound service stables overnight in Inverness to form the next day's southbound train. The luxury Royal Scotsman train which is powered by locomotives from the West Coast Railway fleet is also a frequent visitor to the route in the summer months.

During daylight hours DB Schenker operate the Stobart Intermodal service in both directions between Mossend and Inverness and Direct Rail Services (DRS) have a southbound Malcolm Intermodal train from Inverness to Coatbridge. Freightliner visit the line on Thursdays with an Inverness to Oxwellmains empty cement train and Friday evenings sees the returning fuel tanks from Lairg to Mossend powered by a DB Schenker Class 66.

During the leaf fall season a Rail Head Treatment Train (RHTT) operates on the line based at Inverness which in autumn 2009 was worked by a single DB Schenker Class 67.

In recent years DRS has outbased a Class 37 at Inverness over the winter months to act as a snowplough over the various routes radiating from Inverness.

Traffic levels are quite low on the Highland route, but the short Scottish nights in the summer months do allow for some photography in the early morning and late evenings with some spectacular scenery as back drops. With the A9 trunk road paralleling the line over most of its route accessing locations is relatively easy. ∎

Above: *Kingussie signal box controls the loop and level crossing at the adjacent station. Since this photograph was taken in August 2005, the box has been extended towards the platform on the upper level and platform level cabinet removed.* **Chris Perkins**

Left: *National Express-liveried Class 43 No. 43320 leads the 07.55 Inverness to London King's Cross past Crubenmore between Newtonmore and Dalwhinnie 30 May 2009.* **Neil Gibson**

Below: *On 3 January 2010, following the failure of the booked HST set with power cars Nos. 43318 and 43307, the retimed 1Z16 13.00 Inverness to Edinburgh departed from the Highland capital behind the resident snowplough locomotive DRS Class 37 No. 37667. It is captured shortly after departure from Invernes. On arrival at Perth, Class 67 No. 67025 took over for the remainder of the journey to Edinburgh.* **Neil MacQueen**

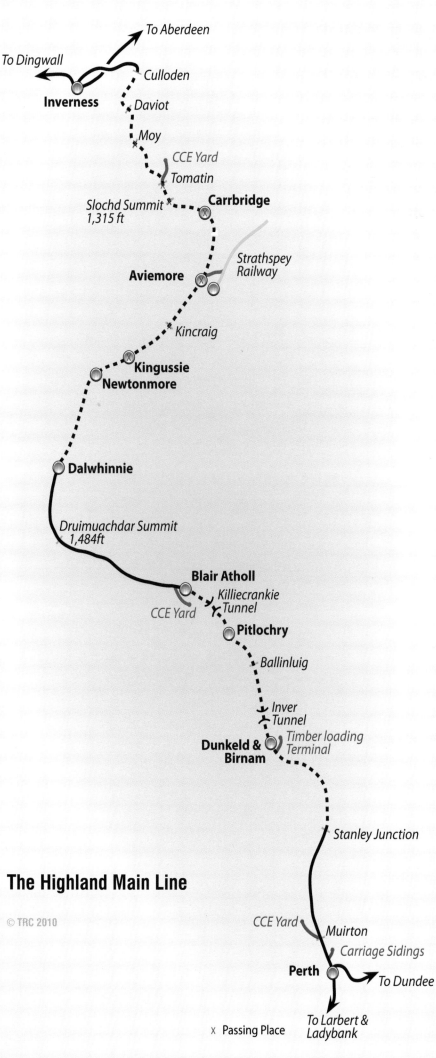

To Aberdeen

To Dingwall

Inverness

Culloden

Daviot

Moy

CCE Yard

Tomatin

Carrbridge

Slochd Summit
1,315 ft

*Strathspey
Railway*

Aviemore

Kincraig

Kingussie
Newtonmore

Dalwhinnie

*Druimuachdar Summit
1,484ft*

Blair Atholl

*Killiecrankie
Tunnel*

CCE Yard

Pitlochry

Ballinluig

*Inver
Tunnel*

*Timber loading
Terminal*

**Dunkeld &
Birnam**

Stanley Junction

The Highland Main Line

© TRC 2010

CCE Yard

Muirton

Carriage Sidings

Perth

To Dundee

To Larbert &
Ladybank

X Passing Place

Above: *Looking south towards Dalwhinnie
at Crubenmore, we see West Coast Railway
Co Class 47 No. 47804 heading a Scottish
Railway Preservation Society's charter from
Dunbar to Kyle of Lochalsh on 30 May 2009.*
Neil Gibson

Right: *The 09.24 Inverness to Coatbridge
intermodal service, formed of just four
containers, is seen in stunning autumn light
as it passes Moy powered by Direct Rail
Services Class 37s Nos.* **37688 Kingmoor
TMD** *and* **37087 Keighley & Worth Valley
Railway** *on 6 October 2009.* **Roddy MacPhee**

Left Top: *Direct Rail Services Class 66/4 No. 66412 in Malcolm Rail livery is seen just after crossing Culloden viaduct with train 4N47, the 13.22 Inverness to Grangemouth Stobart Rail intermodal service on 26 September 2009.* Roddy MacPhee

Right Top: *Stobart Rail liveried Class 66 No. 66048* **James the Engine** *stands in Needlefield Yard, Inverness on the first day of DB Schenker operating the Stobart Rail service on 4 January 2010. This train later crashed at Carrbridge following brake problems on the descent from Slochd summit, and thus this is one of the few pictures of this Stobart Rail-liveried loco powering the Stobart train.* Steven Robertson

Right Middle: *Turbostar Class 170 No. 170421 arrives at Aviemore on 3 August 2005, forming the 07.10 Glasgow Queen Street to Inverness service. The line in the foreground is the connection to the Strathspey Railway, and is used by the Royal Scotsman VIP charter service.* Chris Perkins

Left Bottom: *DRS Class 66/4 No. 66429 slowly approaches Perth station on 31 December 2009 powering train 4Z50, the 09.24 Inverness to Coatbridge intermodal service.* Steven Robertson

Below: *Freightliner Class 66/6 No. 66615 waits in the loop at Slochd summit with train 6B31, the 17.00 Inverness to Oxwellmains empty cement tanks on 8 October 2009. Approaching off the single line is DBS Class 67 No. 67004 powering the Inverness-based Rail Head Treatment Train.* Roddy MacPhee

Left Top: *The Inverness to Grangemouth Stobart Rail service powered by DRS Class 66/4 No. 66420 crosses Alt-na-Slanach viaduct at Moy on 10 April 2009. This listed structure still has the original timbers but has been strengthened in the centre.* **Roddy MacPhee**

Right Top: *BR InterCity-liveried Class 37s Nos. 37683 and 37510 cross Findhorn viaduct at Tomatin with the Inverness to London Euston sleeper service heading for the summit at Slochd on 5 June 1994.* **Chris Perkins**

Right Middle: *With yet another heavy fall of snow over Scotland at the end of February 2010, Monday 1 March 2010 saw DRS Class 37s Nos. 37510 and 37218 at work on the Highland Main Line with the Inverness-based independent snowploughs climbing to Slochd summit at Carrbridge. It is interesting to note that No. 37510 is still at work on the line 16 years after the above picture was taken.* **Roddy MacPhee**

Left Bottom: *Direct Rail Services Class 66/4 No. 66427 approaches Cradlehall crossover near Inverness on 13 March 2009, powering train 4H47, the 05.00 from Grangemouth to Inverness 'Stobart Rail' service.* **Donald Stirling**

Below: *Turbostar Class 170 No. 170434 has departed from Dalwhinnie and passes the whisky distillery of the same name on 25 May 2008. The three-car Derby-built set is forming the 13.50 Edinburgh to Inverness.* **Alan Mitchell**

Above: *The Royal Scotsman empty stock arrives at Aviemore on 8 June 2008 behind West Coast Railway Class 47 No. 47826. The passengers would have detrained at Carrbridge and been taken on a coach tour of the Highlands. The stock will be reversed onto the Strathspey Railway and taken to Boat of Garten by the railway's Class 31 where the passengers will rejoin the train for an overnight stay and return to Aviemore next morning. The Class 47 stables on the connecting link with the National Network overnight.* **Steven Robertson**

Below: *West Coast Railway-owned Class 57 No. 57601 heads north through the gorge at Killiecrankie on 8 May 2004 with an empty stock move between Pitlochry and Blair Atholl. This was the first visit of a Class 57 to the Highland Main Line.* **Neil Gibson**

Above: *Class 170 No. 170411, painted in First ScotRail-livery, has just departed from Dunkeld forming the 16.11 Glasgow Queen Street to Inverness service on 30 May 2009. The portal of Inver tunnel can be seen in the background. Apart from the daily HST, sleeper service and charter trains the Class 170s are staple passenger traction for the Highland Line.* **Neil Gibson**

Below: *Following re-instatement earlier in 2009 for railtour duties, DBS Class 37/5 No. 37670* **St Blazey T&RS Depot** *was also used for ballast workings over the Scottish lines. On 25 June 2009 it is seen crossing Slochd viaduct returning empty ballast wagons from a possession at Achnasheen to Carlisle. This locomotive was later painted into DB red livery.* **Neil Gibson**

Yellow is the colour

By Colin J. Marsden

Until the mid-1990s privatisation of the UK railways, the research, development and track assessment was carried out by various departments based at the Railway Technical Centre in Derby.

Following the separation of the track infrastructure from the train operators (passenger and freight), the track owner originally Railtrack, later Network Rail took over the responsibility for its own track and infrastructure inspection, building up a sizeable fleet of mainly ex revenue earning coaches specially adapted to perform specialist inspection rolls.

Power for these test and inspection trains came from several sources, including the national freight operators and the smaller private companies such as FM Rail, Fragonset and Rail Vehicle Engineering.

Network Rail did however eventually take over the operation of a small locomotive fleet to power such trains, mainly the universal Brush-built Class 31.

The quest to provide a higher speed track inspection process to enable a test train to fit in with normal passenger schedules saw the development and introduction of the New Measurement Train (NMT), utilizing a pair of Class 43 HST power cars with various Mk3 test cars marshalled between. This train has a strict operating schedule and patrols the entire UK main line rail network on a timetabled basis, with a greater concentration of activity on the West Coast Main Line.

With the development of the European Railway Traffic Management System (ERTMS) where the display of trackside signals have

been brought into the driving cab, four Class 37s were rebuilt with Network Rail funding as trial and development locos numbered in the 973xx series and are now fitted with full cab signalling, they usually operate from Shrewsbury over the Cambrian Coast route.

The vast majority of these Network Rail test and trial vehicles are painted in high-visibility yellow, many of often blank-faced coaches are seen by enthusiasts and the general public who have little or no idea of what these items of rolling stock do and what original vehicles they were converted from.

In recent years a major development in the operation of Network Rail test trains has been the introduction of converted Mk2 DBSO vehicles as remote driving cars, enabling one locomotive to operate at one end of the train

with full driving controls at the remote end.

Most test vehicles seen today are modified from ex-passenger stock with a very few purpose built, however, the rebuilding work undertaken, usually at Derby has completely changed the appearance of some coaches, frequently grilles are inserted into body sides to provide ventilation for on-board generators and windows plated over.

A purpose built Class 150 'Sprinter' outline two-car DMU was introduced in the 1980s as a track assessment unit, replacing older first generation stock, originally operated by BR this set is now under Network Rail ownership.

The Plasser-built Eurorailscout twin DMU set was also operated in the UK in the early years of this century until exported to mainland Europe in late 2009. ∎

Above: Network Rail-liveried No. 31285 propels the track assessment train formed of former inspection saloon No. 999508, now modified as a hauled vehicle and led by Mk2f DBSO No. 9701. The train is seen passing Chittening Warth on the Severn Beach branch on 20 July 2009. Note the Second Severn Crossing in the background. **Chris Perkins**

Above: *Three days after the picture was taken on the previous page, the same formation of DBSO No. 9701, inspection coach No. 999508 and Class 31 No. 31285 depart from Paignton bound for Newton Abbot. The original gangway doors have been completely removed from the NR-operated DBSOs.* **Nathan Williamson**

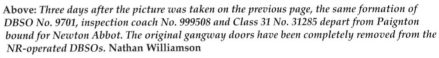

Below & Left: *The guarantee that lineside structures owned by the railway or adjacent land owners infringe on a strict gauge envelope a structure gauging train is operated over all main lines. Usually powered by a Class 31, the four vehicle set includes 4-wheel vehicle DC460000 (left) which 'fires' laser light at structures to measure their position. The train usually operates at night with the gauging car and adjacent portions of the support coaches painted matt black to avoid light reflection during measuring. Top and tailed by Nos. 31285 and 31106 the train passes Cockwood on 27 March 2007 forming a transit move to Penzance.* **CJM**

Fact File – The Network Rail 'Yellow Fleet' Coaching Stock

Number	Design	Type	Livery
1256 (3296)	Mk2f	Support coach	Network Rail yellow
5981	Mk2f	Support coach	Network Rail yellow
6261	Mk1	Generator van	Network Rail yellow
6262	Mk1	Generator van	Network Rail yellow
6263	Mk1	Generator van	Network Rail yellow
6264	Mk1	Generator van	Network Rail yellow
9481	Mk2d	Support coach	Network Rail yellow
9701	Mk2f	DBSO	Network Rail yellow
9702	Mk2f	DBSO	Network Rail yellow
9703	Mk2f	DBSO	Network Rail yellow
9708	Mk2f	DBSO	Network Rail yellow
9714	Mk2f	DBSO	Network Rail yellow
68501 (61281)	EMU	De-icing vehicle	Network Rail yellow
68504 (61286)	EMU	De-icing vehicle	Network Rail yellow
68505 (61299)	EMU	De-icing vehicle	Network Rail yellow
68508 (61272)	EMU	De-icing vehicle	Network Rail yellow
73612	Mk2f	Brake force runner	Network Rail Blue
72616	Mk2f	Brake force runner	Network Rail yellow
72630	Mk2f	Brake force runner	Network Rail yellow
72631	Mk2f	Brake force runner	Network Rail yellow
72639	Mk2f	Brake force runner	Network Rail yellow
99666 (3250)	Mk2e	Ultrasonic test coach	Network Rail yellow
975081 (35313)	Mk1	Structure gauging coach	Network Rail yellow
975091 (34615)	Mk1	Overhead line test coach	Network Rail yellow
975280 (21263)	Mk1	Staff coach	Network Rail yellow
975464 (35171)	Mk1	Snowblower support coach	Network Rail yellow
975481 (34606)	Mk1	Generator coach	Network Rail yellow
975486 (34100)	Mk1	Snowblower support coach	Network Rail yellow
975494 (35082)	Mk1	Re-railing train (MG)	Departmental yellow
975573 (34729)	Mk1	Re-railing train (MG)	Departmental yellow
975574 (34599)	Mk1	Re-railing train (TO)	Departmental yellow
975611 (68201)	Mk1	Re-railing train (TO)	Departmental yellow
975612 (68203)	Mk1	Re-railing train (MG)	Departmental yellow
975613 (68202)	Mk1	Re-railing train (TO)	Departmental yellow
975814 (41000)	Mk3	Conference coach	Network Rail yellow
975984 (40000)	Mk3	Lecture coach	Network Rail yellow
977088 (34990)	Mk1	Generator coach	Network Rail yellow
977107 (21202)	Mk1	Re-railing train (SP)	Network Rail yellow
977235 (34989)	MK1	Re-railing train (SP)	Network Rail yellow
977337 (9395)	Mk2	Staff coach	Network Rail yellow
977868 (5846)	Mk2e	Radio survey coach	Network Rail yellow
977869 (5858)	Mk2e	Radio survey coach	Network Rail yellow
977969 (2906)	Mk2	Staff coach	Network Rail yellow
977974 (5854)	Mk2e	Laboratory coach	Network Rail yellow
977983 (72503)	Mk2f	Hot box detection coach	Network Rail yellow
977984 (40501)	Mk3	Staff coach	Network Rail yellow
977985 (72715)	Mk2f	Brake force runner	Network Rail yellow
977986 (3189)	Mk2d	Track recording coach	Network Rail yellow
977993 (44053)	Mk3	Overhead line test coach	Network Rail yellow
977994 (44087)	Mk3	Track recording coach	Network Rail yellow
977995 (40719)	Mk3	Generator coach	Network Rail yellow
977996 (44062)	Mk3	Battery coach for 43089	Network Rail yellow
977997 (72613)	Mk2f	Radio survey coach	Network Rail yellow
999508	Saloon	Track recording coach (UTU3)	Network Rail yellow
999550	Mk2	Track recording coach	Network Rail yellow
999602 (62483)	Mk1	Ultrasonic test coach (UTU3)	Network Rail yellow
999605 (62482)	Mk1	Ultrasonic test coach (UTU2)	Network Rail yellow
999606 (62356)	Mk1	Ultrasonic test coach (UTU4)	Network Rail yellow

Below: Two purpose-built Class 150/1 outline DMU cars were fabricated at BREL York Works in 1977 to lot numbers 4060 and 4061 for a purpose built state-of-the-art track assessment unit. The two coaches, one a near normal passenger coach and one an instrumentation vehicle, were fitted out at the Engineering Development Unit (EDU) at the Derby Railway Technical Centre. After a period of working for BR in blue and grey departmental livery, the set as No. 950001 passed to Railtrack (Network Rail) on privatisation and now sports all over yellow livery. With some extra fittings such as lamps, cameras and jumpers on the nose end, the snowplough fitted set is seen passing adjacent to the Dawlish Sea Wall at Rockstone on 5 April 2007 with a St Blazey to Bristol track inspection run. CJM

Above: *In 2003 Plasser & Theurer introduced a UFM160 two-car track inspection set, with vehicles numbered 999700 and 999701, the set known as Eurorailscout was operated by Network Rail until 2009 when the set was transferred to Mainland Europe. The UFM160 operated mainly in the south of the UK and East Anglia. On 13 April 2009, the Plasser twin-set is seen passing West Hatch near Tisbury on the Salisbury to Exeter main line.* **Steve King**

Below: *Operator Direct Rail Services, based in Carlisle have a contract to provide power for a number of Network Rail test trains. Usually the company provide Class 37s to power these trains, often in pairs in a top and tail formation. In this 17 August 2009 view DRS 'Compass'-liveried Nos. 37602 and 37218 sandwich four immaculate Network Rail yellow Mk2s forming a radio survey train operating from Derby RTC to Bristol Temple Meads via Newport, seen passing Pilning and approaching the Severn Tunnel. The train is formed of 9481 a former Mk2d BSO, 977997 the radio survey coach which was rebuilt from former Gatwick Express TSOLH No. 72613 and was originally Mk2f TSO No. 6126, Mk2f RFB No. 1256, originally an FO No. 3296 now a test train support and make up vehicle and Mk2f TSO No. 5981 another make up and support vehicle.* **Chris Perkins**

NR Yellow Traction Units

The following locomotives and power cars are in operation with Network Rail and in mid-2010 were painted in yellow livery.

Locomotives

Number	Home Depot/ Poole	Use
31105	DF/QADD	Test train power
31233	DF/QADD	Test train power
31285	DF/QADD	Test train power
31465	DF/QADD	Test train power
37198	BH/MBDL	Test train power
43013	EC/QCAR	NMT power
43014	EC/QCAR	NMT power
43062	EC/QCAR	NMT power
73138	DF/QAED	Test train power
86901	RU/QACL	Load Bank
86901	RU/QACL	Load bank
97301	BH/QETS	ERTMS power
97302	BH/QETS	ERTMS power
97303	BH/QETS	ERTMS power
97304	BH/QETS	ERTMS power

Multiple Units

Number	Home Depot/ Poole	Use
950001	QTRU	Track Assessment

The following locomotives are owned by Rail Vehicle Engineering Ltd and operated on Network Rail trains.
31106, 31454, 31459, 31468, 31601, 31602. Several of these are painted in un-branded yellow livery.

Below: The radio survey train illustrated with the DRS power on the previous page, visited the Bristol area again on 18 November 2009. This time the power was provided by a pair of Network Rails own Class 31s, painted in full yellow livery, Nos. 31285 and electric train supply fitted No. 31465. The pair are seen 'top and tail' of train 1Z12 from Derby to Bristol passing Dr Days Junction. The train is again formed of vehicles Nos. 5981, 1256, 977997 and 9481. Note how the cab end of the Class 31 has been modified for its Network Rail role, with the fitting of five high intensity lights (three at roof height and two above the buffer beam on special support brackets). A central camera has also been fitted behind the original nose end communicating doors, looking forward through a new slit mid-height in the central panel.
Chris Perkins

Above: The most significant change to the operation of track test trains in the UK was the introduction of the New Measurement Train or NMT in 2003. The set, through various test cars can assess the condition of the track and even overhead power contact wire and determine where work is required. The train measures the contact between the wheel and rail and checks track geometry, overhead line height and stagger, track gauge rail twist and cant. Cameras on the front and rear record the route in precise detail with extra cameras recording the pantograph (when raised) and the wheel/rail interface. Equipment on board can also detect if a single rail clip is out of place! On 20 April 2009 the NMT, led by power car No. 43014 is seen traversing the Settle and Carlisle line at Ais Gill viaduct with a Heaton to Derby run. Richard Armstrong

Right: Led by power-car No. 43013 with No. 43067 bringing up the rear, track test train 1B00 from Swindon to Swansea passes a Network Rail track gang working on the new crossovers at Magor between Severn tunnel Junction and Newport on 25 November 2005. In 2009-10 the three NMT power cars were all refurbished by Brush Traction to incorporate the latest MTU power units. Chris Perkins

Left: 999606 *The ultrasonic testing on the rail tracks is a very important operation to ensure the safe operation of trains at high speeds. Network Rail operate three UTU (Ultrasonic Test Units) to ensure track conditions are perfect. The test vehicles in each set are heavily rebuilt former Southern Region EMU motor brake vehicles. Vehicle No. 999606 is illustrated, this was rebuilt from the MBSO from Class 421 (4-CIG) coach 62356, which originally operated in set 7368 when new in 1970 and later in renumbered sets 1268 and latterly 1850. The coach was totally rebuilt for its Ultrasonic role, with a roller shutter door in the former brake end, underslung tanks and specially modified recording bogies which are illuminated by high-powered frame mounted lights when in operation.* Nathan Williamson

Right: 999550 *One of the few purpose-built track test cars of the modern era was Mk2f-design vehicle No. 999550, built in 1977 by BREL Derby and was thus the final Mk2 coach built for BR. The 64ft 6in long vehicle, mounted on B4 bogies has non-standard body profiles and after shell completion at BREL was transferred to the RTC Derby for fitting out. The coach is officially a Track Recording Coach and was originally operated by BR and worked attached to service trains, special services or even within an HST. After privatisation the vehicle became part of the Network Rail fleet and repainted in yellow. In the early years of the New Measurement Train, the coach was formed within this set, but is now used as part of a loco-hauled test formation.* Nathan Williamson

Left: 999508 *This vehicle was built at BR Swindon Works in 1962 as part of a batch of Divisional Engineers Inspection saloons for the Western Region to diagram number 1/552 under lot No. 3379. No. 999508 was the West of England saloon for many years firstly painted in maroon and then blue grey before being withdrawn and taken over by Serco as a hauled track recording coach. Some structural modifications were undertaken and today the vehicle is painted in standard Network Rail yellow and based at the RTC Derby. The vehicle is operated either within another test train with make up vehicles or top and tailed by locomotives.* Nathan Williamson

Right: 977996 *As part of the Hitachi, Brush, Porterbrook and Network Rail dual power project using a HST power car to operate either from its own diesel engine or from a secondary battery pack, this former TGS No. 44062 was heavily rebuilt at Brush Traction to incorporate traction batteries and power control equipment for 43089. The coach was coupled directly behind power car No. 43089 with its battery bay nearest the power car, and operated as part of the New Measurement Train. When the trial project was complete the power car was converted for normal use while the battery coach was stored and is currently at Long Marston. In this view it is seen at Carlisle.* Nathan Williamson

Right: 977993 *Another of the New Measurement Train (NMT) vehicles is this pantograph fitted overhead equipment test car. Its pantograph is purely for recording and in no way collects power. The coach, converted from Mk3 TGS No. 44053 is usually maintained in the NMT formation even when working away from the overhead. The special pantograph well was fabricated in the area above the original brake compartment. In common with the entire NMT set, its base is Edinburgh Craigentinny. In this view it is seen at Newton Abbot when working a Plymouth to Paddington test special.* Nathan Williamson

Left: 977986 *Originally built as Mk2d FO No. 3189, this coach was later modified as a SO and numbered 6231. After withdrawal it was taken over and converted as an exhibition coach when it was renumbered as 99664. After withdrawal from this role it was taken over by Network Rail as a support vehicle for the track recording train, having the unusual appearance of slab sides, gained during its use as an exhibition vehicle. The coach is seen at Exeter St Davids.* Nathan Williamson

Right: 977868 *Rebuilt from Mk2e TSO No. 5846, this vehicle is now part of the radio equipment survey train, some structural changes, including the plating over of one side window have been carried out for its departmental role. Note the extra roof mounted equipment at the near end and the high level power jumper on the coach end.* Nathan Williamson

Left: 977969 *This is a coach which has had an interesting career. Built as a Mk2b BFK in 1969 with the number 14112, it was subsequently taken into Royal Train use and renumbered 2906. After this duty ceased it was taken over by Network Rail as a test train staff coach, retaining its window configuration when in Royal use. The vehicle can now be found working within different test train formations.* Nathan Williamson

Left: 975280 *This is a Mk1 vehicle which has seen lots of different users during its departmental career. Rebuilt in 1973 from Southern Region BCK No. 21263 the vehicle has operated within the structural gauging set for many years and is the train dormitory and generator vehicle. As can be seen some major structural changes have been undertaken since its passenger carrying days. The coach is seen at Bristol Temple Meads.* Nathan Williamson

Right: 975081 *Entering departmental use in 1971, this former Mk1 BSK No. 35313 was originally modified as a driving control car and named* **Hermes***, with a Southern Region VEP style cab end. This front was retained for many years under the remit of BR Research, when it was allocated to the structure gauging train. Today the vehicle is semi-permanantly coupled to structure gauging laser car DC460000 and has that end of the vehicle painted matt black. This view shows the original cab end, the cab door and handrails have been retained while the side and front windows have been plated over. In recent years some of the bodyside windows have been removed.* Nathan Williamson

Left: 9708 *Former Edinburgh-Glasgow DBSO No. 9708, rebuilt from BSO No. 9530 is one of five DBSOs now operated by Network Rail. All have specific roles, with the vehicle illustrated being part of the structure gauging train with its inner end painted matt black and coupled to the optical test car. These vehicles have full driving controls and can operate with any of the test-centre motive power. This vehicle also has a small generator located to the rear of the cab end vestibule.* Nathan Williamson

Right: 72630 *After withdrawal from passenger use on the Gatwick Express service following introduction of Class 460 EMUs, a number of the two and three-car semi-permanantly formed Class 488 sets saw departmental use, some with Network Rail. Five vehicles were in stock in 2010 officially classified as Test Train Brake Force Runners and are marshalled within test train formations to increase brake efficiency or to provide enough coaches in a formation to allow higher speed operation. Car No. 72630 is illustrated at Carlisle, this was modified from a Gat-Ex Class 488/3 and was prior to that Mk2f TSO No. 6094.* Nathan Williamson

Above: *To enable dynamic testing of the trial installation of the European Railway Traffic Management System (ERTMS), Network Rail required four locomotives to be fully equipped and operate over the Cambrian Line in Wales. Four Class 37s were selected and after conversion at Barrow Hill these became classified as 97/3 and numbered 97301-97304, carrying full Network Rail livery. No. 97301 is seen crossing the River Severn at Caersws powering the 11.58 Aberystwyth to Shrewsbury on 4 June 2009.* **Richard Jones**

Below: *In 2004, Network Rail purchased three Class 86/2 locomotives Nos. 86210/253/424, two (86210/ 253) have since been converted at Barrow Hill into mobile load-bank locomotives. The two operational locos were reclassified as Class 86/9, and renumbered 86901/902. They are currently allocated to Rugby, but spend time at Crewe, Derby and York. Both carry Network Rail all-over yellow livery. These locos primary use is to test 25kV ac overhead power supply by simulating various loads. They are capable of running under their own power (one bogie retains traction equipment) for positioning purposes, but cannot haul any significant load. No. 86901* **Chief Engineer***, is seen passing Carnforth on 9 August 2006.* **Mark Bearton**

The British Royal Train

By Colin J. Marsden

One of the most impressive trains to operate in the UK is the Royal Train, thankfully through several transport reviews of Royal Travel, we have managed to retain this often mysterious train of dark coaches with curtains drawn which is seen by many who have no idea what the train is.

UK Royal Train travel dates back to 13 June 1842, when Queen Victoria travelled by Royal Train, operated by the Great Western Railway from Paddington to Windsor. After the death of Queen Victoria, her casket was transported by Royal Train from London to Windsor, this setting up the precedence for all subsequent monarchs, and one which will continue to at least the death of Queen Elizabeth II.

Until rail Nationalisation each railway and company operated its own Royal Train, which continued largely with the BR Regions and it was not until 1977 that the UK saw one unified Royal Train. This was formed of a variety of vehicles from different companies and vastly improved prior to 1977 when the Queen used the train for an extensive tour of the UK.

New modified Mk2 and 3 stock was added to the Royal Train fleet in the 1970s and 1980s and today we have a fleet of nine vehicles with two stored spares.

The Royal Train is kept and maintained at Wolverton near Milton Keynes by a dedicated team of depot and operational staff. The train is used around 15-20 times every year and presently only available for use by the Queen, Prince Philip, Prince Charles and the Duchess of Cornwall. Until recently other members of

There can be few more impressive locations to capture the Royal Train than on the picturesque Dawlish Sea Trall. On 11 September 2009, the full Royal set, led by No. 67005 hauling Royal Stock Nos. 2921, 2922, 2923, 2916, 2917, 2915 and 2920 together with Class 67 No. 67006 on the rear, approaches Rockstone Bridge. The train, complete with Welsh flags, was operating as the 09.33 Newton Abbot to Exeter 'Royal Special' carrying the Prince of Wales for a days engagements in Exeter. The train on this occasion travelled slowly between Teignmouth and Dawlish Warren to allow the Prince to see the rough sea. CJM

the senior Royal Family were able to use the train, but on cost grounds this has now stopped.

Motive power for the Royal Train was until privatisation provided by the operating region, from privatisation, English Welsh and Scottish Railway, now DB Schenker are the providers of traction and train crew. In the 1990s a pair of Class 47s were dedicated to Royal Train use and repainted in Royal Claret livery. With traction modernisation in the post privatisation years a pair of Class 67s Nos. 67005/006 are now repainted in Royal Claret livery and made

available when required to power the Royal set. When not required for this purpose the locos are used in the general Class 67 fleet.

When the Royal Train is operated it is usually formed of between six and eight coaches, depending on the role it is playing and for operational reasons is 'top and tailed' by the two dedicated Class 67s.

In the future it has been suggested that a Mk3 DVT will be made available to operate with the Royal set, to reduce the loco operating costs. ∎

Above: During the 1960s and 70s when regional traction was used to power the Royal Train, a pair of immaculate English Electric Type 4 Class 40s were frequently used, often specially prepared by Crewe depot. With disc headcode No. 40025 nearest the camera, the full Royal set passes Northampton No. 2 signalbox bound for the Royal Train base at Wolverton on 3 May 1977. Robin Patrick

Below: With a superb collection of Mk2, Mk3 and vintage Royal Train stock, Stratford Class 47/4 No. 47585 **County of Cambridgeshire** approaches York past Dringhouses on 16 September 1986. At the time some members of the lower Royal Household were still eligible to use the Royal Train, on this occasion the main passenger was the Duchess of Kent. Robin Patrick

Above: In pristine condition English Electric Type 4 No. D384 painted in 1960s BR green with a small yellow warning panel, passes Roade Junction Signal Box (located behind the locomotive) at 07.00 on 1 July 1964 powering Royal Special 1X01 from Edinburgh Princes Street to London Euston, conveying HM The Queen and other members of the Royal Household. Note the cable on the front of the loco which connected to the Royal stock to provide voice communication between train and locomotive. Robin Patrick

Below: Class 25s were also popular power for the Royal Train in the 1960s-70s, where clean boiler fitted examples were frequently to be found powering the train, especially on the London Midland Region. On 25 May 1976, two unidentified Class 25s in rail-blue livery power a five vehicle Royal set just south of Northampton Station and crossing the River Nene viaduct. Robin Patrick

Above: *Around one hour after the picture on the opening spread of this feature was taken on 11 September 2009, the Royal Train again traversed the Dawlish Sea Wall, running as an empty stock move from Exeter St Davids to Hackney Yard, Newton Abbot. In some very rough sea conditions the train passes slowly adjacent to Marine Parade - hopefully all the windows were tightly closed!* CJM

Right: *The cast 'By Appointment' badge applied to Royal Class 67s Nos. 67005 and 67006.* Chris Perkins

By Appointment to
Her Majesty The Queen
Royal Train Operator
English Welsh & Scottish Railway Ltd
London

The Royal Train Passenger Fleet - Post 1977

Number	Former Number	Type	Date Introduced	Livery	Internal Layout	Notes/Disposal
2900	-	-	1955	-	Royal Family Lounge, Bedroom and Bathroom	Preserved at Fawley Hill Railway
2901	-	-	1957	-	Royal Household, Office, Bedroom, Bathroom	Preserved at Bressingham Museum
2902	(499)	-	1956	-	Royal Family Dining Car and Kitchen	Preserved Midland Railway, renumbered 1977
2903	(11001)	AT5G	1977	ROY	HM The Queen's Saloon	Part of current train
2904	(12001)	AT5G	1977	ROY	HRH The Duke of Edinburgh's Saloon	Part of current train
2905	(14105)	BFK	1977	-	Royal Household Couchette, Generator and Brake	Returned to National fleet then to Riviera Trains
2906	(14112)	BFK	1977	-	Royal Household Corchette	Returned to National fleet as DB977969 Generator Van
2907	(325)	PFK	1977	-	Royal Household Dining and Kitchen	Returned to National fleet as 325, then to VSOE(N)
2908	(2013)	SLF	1977	-	Royal Household Sleeper	Preserved at Southall Railway Museum
2909	(2500)	SLS	1981	-	Royal Household Sleeper	Disposed by West Coast Railway Co, Carnforth
2910	(M31209M)	Spl	1941	-	Royal Household Sleeper	Scrapped 1991, renumbered 1983
2911	(M45000M)	Spl	1941	-	Special Saloon	Preserved Midland Railway, renumbered from LNWR5000
2912	(M45006M)	Spl	1942	-	Special Saloon	Scrapped 1991, renumbered 1983
2913	Number not used					
2914	(10734)	SLE	1985	-	Royal Household Sleeper	Returned to BR as 10734, now with VSOE(N)
2915	(10735)	AT5G	1985	ROY	Royal Household Sleeping Coach	Part of current train
2916	(40512)	AT5G	1986	ROY	HRH The Prince of Wales's Dining Coach	Part of current train
2917	(40514)	AT5G	1986	ROY	Kitchen Car and Royal Household Dining Coach	Part of current train
2918	(40515)	AT5G	1986	ROY	Royal Household Coach	Stored at Wolverton
2919	(40518)	AT5G	1986	ROY	Royal Household Coach	Stored at Wolverton
2920	(17109)	AT5B	1986	ROY	Generator Coach and Household Sleeping Coach	Part of current train
2921	(17107)	AT5B	1986	ROY	Brake, Coffin Carrier and Household Accommodation	Part of current train
2922	-	AT5G	1987	ROY	HRH The Prince of Wales's Sleeping Coach	Part of current train
2923	-	AT5G	1987	ROY	Royal Passenger Saloon	Part of current train

Mk2
Vehicle Length: 66ft 0in (20.11m)
Height: 12ft 9½in (3.89m)
Width: 9ft 3in (2.81m)

Mk 3
Vehicle Length: 75ft 0in (22.86m)
Height: 12ft 9in (3.88m)
Width: 8ft 11in (2.71m)

Vehicles shown in red are in current Royal Train service.   **ROY = Royal Train claret livery**

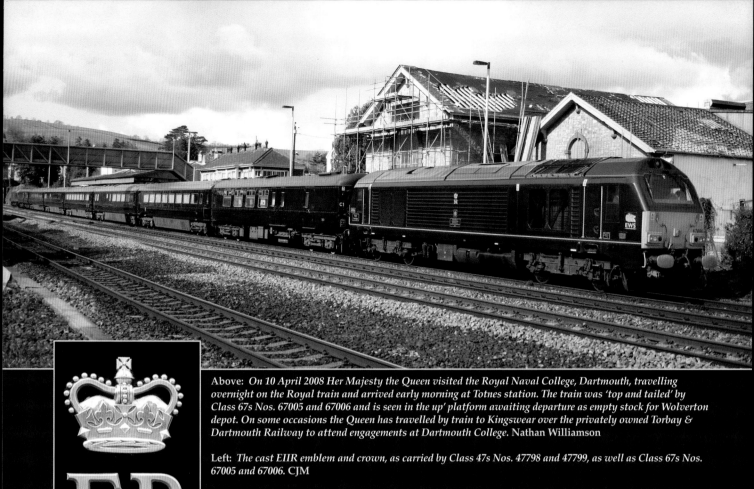

Above: On 10 April 2008 Her Majesty the Queen visited the Royal Naval College, Dartmouth, travelling overnight on the Royal train and arrived early morning at Totnes station. The train was 'top and tailed' by Class 67s Nos. 67005 and 67006 and is seen in the up' platform awaiting departure as empty stock for Wolverton depot. On some occasions the Queen has travelled by train to Kingswear over the privately owned Torbay & Dartmouth Railway to attend engagements at Dartmouth College. Nathan Williamson

Left: The cast EIIR emblem and crown, as carried by Class 47s Nos. 47798 and 47799, as well as Class 67s Nos. 67005 and 67006. CJM

Below: Class 67 No. 67006 is seen bringing up the rear of the Royal Train at Settle Junction on 22 March 2005 when the train was powered northbound over the Settle & Carlisle line by steam loco Duchess of Sutherland. John Whiteley

Above: *In the days when regional traction resources were used to power the Royal Train, this usually meant an ex-works or repainted loco being provided. On 6 February 1987, Stratford depot supplied No. 47585* **County of Cambridgeshire** *to power the Royal Train for an official visit to Bradford. In near perfect lighting conditions the train is seen passing Low Moor.* John Whiteley

Right: *When the Royal Train was allocated its own Class 47/7s Nos. 47798/799 and the pair were repainted in Royal Claret livery in May 1995, cast number plate and a Crewe depot cat logo were applied on the cab side below the drivers side window.* CJM

Below: *Formed of just four coaches, including one BR Inter-City-liveried Mk2, the Royal Train powered by Class 47/4 No. 47574 passes Mill Lane Junction on the approaches to Bradford Interchange on 10 June 1981. The first two vehicles are Nos. M31209M and M45006M, built in 1941/42 for King George VI. These two vehicles were renumbered into the main BR train as Nos. 2910 and 2912 in 1983. The two were withdrawn in 1989.* John Whiteley

The Royal Train Locomotive Fleet

1990-2004 Number	Former Number	Original Name	Revised Name	Into Res Livery	Into EWS livery	Notes
47798	47834, 47609, 47072, D1656	*Fire Fly* (08/85)	*Prince William* (05/95)	May-1995	October 1997	Now preserved at NRM, York
47799	47835, 47620, 47070, D1654	*Windsor Castle* (07/85)	*Prince Henry* (05/95)	May-1995	October 1997	

2004-2010 Number	Former Number	Name	Into Res Livery	Notes
67005	-	*Queen's Messenger* (12/00)	February-2004	
67006	-	*Royal Sovereign* (02/05)	January 2005	
67029	-	*Royal Diamond* (10/07)		Stand-by Royal loco, painted in EWS/DBS VIP silver livery

Above: Looking immaculate in EWS Royal Train livery, Nos. 47799 and 47798 stand side by side in the yard at Wolverton on 11 May 1995. Note the additional RCH jumper on the front end to give communication between loco and train. CJM

Below: Frequently, when the Royal Train is required to arrive at a destination early in the morning, it will depart from London the previous evening and recess overnight at one of several overnight stabling locations, where good access can be provided to the train, while security can be maintained. After recessing at Heathfield, the Royal heads west to Totnes at Aller on 10 April 1997. The Queen's lounge is nearest the camera. CJM

Prince William

The two cast 'Prince' nameplates, applied to Class 47s Nos. 47798 and 47799 fom May 1995. Both: CJM

Prince Henry

Left: 2919 A vehicle which is no longer officially in the active Royal fleet, this coach was introduced in 1989 as part of the modernised Mk3 set, it was rebuilt by Wolverton Works from 1976 built HST TRUK No. 40518. This vehicle was converted as a Royal Household kitchen and riding saloon. It was converted under lot No. 31085, mounted on BT10 bogies, with an ETS index of 10X and weighs 41.5 tonnes. CJM

Right: 2916 Introduced in 1986 as part of the modernised Mk3 Royal Train, this vehicle was rebuilt by Wolverton from 1976 built HST TRUK No. 40512, which had been made redundant due to HST catering stock changes. This vehicle is sometimes referred to as the Prince of Wales Dining Car. It retains a large kitchen at one end, with the passenger area opened out with a central longitudinal table with seating for 14. The coach is air conditioned, mounted on BT10 bogies, has an ETS index of 13X and weighs 43 tonnes. The vehicle is shown from the saloon end.
Nathan Williamson

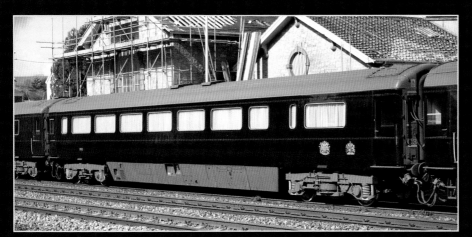

Left: 2923 Built new in 1987, using a coach body produced at BREL Derby and fitted out at Wolverton Works, this is the Prince of Wales's saloon. Based on a standard Mk3, some special window configurations are included. BT10 bogies are fitted and the coach has an ETS index of 7X and weighs 43.2 tonnes. Nathan Williamson

Below: 2903 Rebuilt from prototype HST FO No. 11001, this is the Queens lounge, bedroom, bathroom and office vehicle. It is used for all State occasions and has a double leaf inward opening door at one end. The Queens cypher is carried on both sides below the first window from the left end. The coach is mounted on BT10 bogies, has an ETS index of 9X and weighs 36 tonnes.
Nathan Williamson

Above: 2917 *Rebuilt by Wolverton Works in 1986, this is a Royal Household kitchen and dining car. It was rebuilt from 1977 BREL Derby built HST TRUK No. 40514. Seating in the saloon is for 22 in the conventional 2+1 style. BT10 bogies are fitted, the coach weighs 43 tonnes and has an ETS index of 13X to cover the electric cooking equipment.* Nathan Williamson

Right: 2915 *Rebuilt from Mk3 sleeping car No. 10735 at Wolverton in 1985, with some window changes on both sides, this is the Royal Household sleeping car, it can sleep 12 in separate compartments and has two toilets and a shower compartment. The coach is mounted on BT10 bogies, has an ETS index of 11X and weighs 44 tonnes.* Nathan Williamson

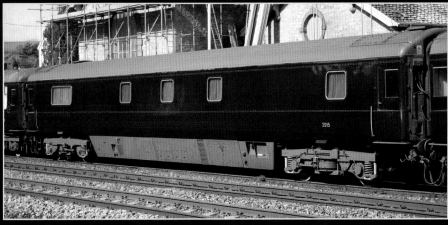

Left: 2920 *Rebuilt by Wolverton Works in 1989-90 to lot number 31044 from 1969 Derby-built Mk2b BFK No. 17109 (14109), this coach is officially a Royal Household couchette, generator and brake vehicle. The brake contains a 350kW generator set for train supply when not attached to a locomotive. The coach had luggage space, a workshop and seating area for train staff. A roof hatch exists above the diesel generator to allow removal. Underfloor fuel tanks are fitted. The coach is mounted on B5 bogies, has an ETS index of 2X and weighs 48 tonnes.* Nathan Williamson

Right: 2921 *Rebuilt by Wolverton Works in 1989-90 to lot number 31086 from 1969 Derby-built Mk2b BFK No. 17107 (14107), this coach is officially a Royal Household couchette, kitchen and brake vehicle. The brake has a central swivel coffin table, which will be used on a Royal funeral train between London and Windsor. The coach is fitted with electric tail lights, mounted on B5 bogies and has an ETS index of 7X, its registered weight is 41.5 tonnes.* Nathan Williamson

Above: *A seven-car rake of Royal stock 'top and tailed' by Royal 67s Nos. 67005 and 67006 pass Burn on the East Coast Main Line on 10 July 2008 while running empty stock to Wolverton from Harrogate via Leeds. The train had taken a large party to Harrogate, including HM The Queen, The Duke of Edinburgh who attended the 150th Great Yorkshire show, while also on board, The Duke of Kent visited a school in Otley and later the Keighley & Worth Valley Railway. Ron Cover*

Left: *As part of a visit by Her Majesty The Queen and The Duke of Edinburgh to Bristol on 25 February 2005, The Queen was invited by the Chief Executive Officer of EWS Railway Keith Heller to unveil the cast number and nameplate* **Royal Sovereign** *on the cabside of the second Royal-liveried Class 67 No. 67006.* **Chris Perkins**

Below: *On rare occasions the Royal Train operates with just one locomotive, the reliability of the '67' fleet is such that operational problems are rare. On 13 July 2006 No. 67006 passes Colton, York with a Royal working from Euston to Harrogate.* **Ron Cover**

Royal Train Workings

Under present guidelines issued by the UK Government, only Her Majesty the Queen, The Duke of Edinburgh, Prince Charles and The Duchess of Cornwall are authorised to use the Royal Train.

Year on year workings, (calculated May to May)

Year	Number of Trips	Average miles per trip
2003-2004	18	736
2004-2005	19	691
2005-2006	14	700
2006-2007	11	655
2007-2008	19	755
2008-2009	14	696

In the 2008-2009 year, eight trips were undertaken by the Prince of Wales and six by HM The Queen, a total of 19 nights were spend on board the train.

Source - Hansard

Above: Top and tailed by the Royal Class 67s Nos. 67005 and 67006, a seven-car formation of Royal stock slowly climbs Dainton bank between Newton Abbot and Totnes on 10 April 2008, when transporting Her Majesty the Queen to Totnes for a visit to the Royal Naval College, Dartmouth. The train travelled west overnight from London Euston and recessed locally to ensure an on time arrival to the second at Totnes. The timing of the Royal train is exemplary, with Royal Train staff maintaining a near 100 per cent record of on time arrivals, with trains frequently holding back for a few seconds on the approach to its final destination. Nigel Curtis

Below: On 12 May 2009 Her Majesty the Queen and The Duke of Edinburgh visited the South Hook Natural Gas Terminal at Milford Haven, arriving by train at Haverfordwest. After off loading the train returned empty to Wolverton by way of the GW main line to Acton, and then Willesden and the West Coast route. The empty stock move is seen approaching Slough. Motive power is provided by No. 67005, with No. 67006 on the rear. Kim Fullbrook

Royal Train Fact File

- The UK Royal Train is based at the Railcare site at Wolverton, near Milton Keynes - the home of the Royal Train for more than 100 years.
- The Royal Train is owned by Network Rail and operated by DB Schenker.
- The train is usually 'top & tailed' by Class 67s Nos. 67005 and 67006.
- The annual millage of the Royal Train is around 9,500 miles (15,288km).
- The Royal train and its dedicated locos are painted in Royal Claret livery.
- When the Queen dies, she will be conveyed from London to Windsor by Royal Train, with the coffin carried in coach 2921.
- Each Royal train is specially marshalled to meet local requirements with the Royal part having easy access from station entrance to train.
- The present Royal Train was refurbished in 1977 for a nationwide tour by the Queen to mark her Silver Jubilee, extra Mk3 vehicles were added to the train in the mid 1980s.

Diesel Galas - Its all in the planning

By Paul Fuller
Diesel Locomotive Manager, Gloucestershire
Warwickshire Railway

Everyone loves a diesel gala and the enjoyment is heightened when it all works out nicely. However, those who turn up on the day and have a good day out probably do not realise the months of planning that goes into such an event.

I have been involved with the planning of diesel galas at the Gloucester Warwickshire Railway (GWR), Toddington for a number of years and while the final result may seem to vary slightly on each event to cater for all types of enthusiasts – the work that goes on 'behind the scenes' before, during and after each event is just incredible! It just does not simply 'happen' on the day (if only it would!).

The general timetable for the railway (what services and events are on which days) are discussed and agreed by the Commercial Department towards the end of each year for the following year. Several factors are taken into account when deciding which days certain events are held on – perhaps the most important is that of clashes with events on other railways. In respect of diesel galas on other lines, the majority of railways have theirs on roughly the same weekends each year, so we normally get a good idea of who is doing

what and when. Speaking of which, an e-mail discussion group is now being formed with representatives from as many of the heritage railways as possible so that information can be shared much more easily thus preventing any major event clashes – there's nothing worse than sharing your well-planned weekend between two railways and seeing a marked downturn in ticket sales!

Our four main events throughout the year are normally held in March (Spring event to kick the season off), July (Summer event), October (Autumn event) and our traditional Christmas Diesel Day which is held every year on 27 December without fail.

Once the actual dates of events are confirmed, we then form our gala planning committee – which pretty much is made up with a representative from all the diesel locomotive owning groups on the railway, along with one or two members from the Railways' board and if possible, from the Commercial department.

The preliminary meeting is to discuss what plans we have for that year but mainly concentrating on the first event of the year which is an important event for the line as it helps kick the season off in style.

Everything is discussed from the timetable we plan to run (passenger services with possibly some freights) to additional activities

and events, such as the ever-popular 'driver for a fiver', trade stands, lineside photo permits, ticket prices and perhaps most importantly – locomotive availability.

It is normally a rare event for the GWR to hold a diesel gala without all the operational fleet available. Obviously it is understandable if certain locomotives do not appear for an event – such as the Class 73 which has undergone extensive bodywork repairs and a repaint as well as when No. 47376 failed with leaking liners – these things cannot be helped and their non-availability is reported well in advance and also publicised.

Visiting locomotives are vital to keep visitor numbers up on diesel galas, simply for the 'variety' of traction available. At our diesel gala planning meetings, we discuss what locomotives we have had visit us in the past as well as making a 'wish list' of locomotives we would like to invite for an event (or more likely for an entire running season).

Someone from the committee is then charged with approaching loco owning groups with an invite to bring their engines to the GWR for a period of time and arrange follow-up discussions, bringing any information back to the planning committee.

The flip side of this is that sometimes loco owners approach the GWR Diesel Department with a request to bring their locos in and this is

Right: Class 47 No. 47376 **Freightliner 1995** *approaches Hailes overbridge with the 10.00 Winchcombe to Toddington on the 5 November 2006 during the Autumn Diesel Gala.* **Chris Perkins**

Below: Map of the Gloucestershire Warwickshire Railway showing photographic locations, most of which can be accessed from public roads whilst others can only be accessed with a lineside pass which can be obtained from the ticket office at Toddington station for a day pass or by post for an annual pass. The green numbers can be found on the corresponding illustrations in this feature.

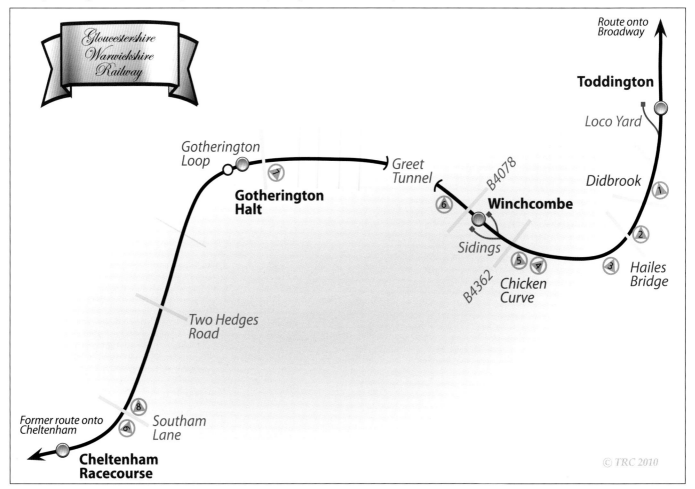

also discussed at our planning meetings and to be honest, very rarely turned down.

The period of time a visiting locomotive will stay varies – we like locomotives to visit for a couple of months as the GWR is not rail connected and road haulage can be quite expensive, especially when the cost is off-set against our income for the event(s) concerned. Various other factors are also taken into account, such as any previous commitments the locomotive owners have outstanding with either their home line or other railways that may have approached them.

Finally, the planning committee take their visiting loco proposal to the Railways' Board who give the green light to arrange the visit.

Once a locomotive line-up is confirmed, the timetable needs to be addressed. The timetables we run on our diesel gala, although generally run along the same pattern each time, are 'tweaked' ever so slightly to make the event slightly different to the last diesel gala – again giving the visitor something different.

With the trains running from Toddington to Cheltenham and back, we are fortunate in that between these we can run two 'shuttles' to Winchcombe and back. However, with Gotherington loop in the final stages of being commissioned, we have looked at draft timetables for future galas and while we can only run to Cheltenham and back seven times in one day at present, we will soon be able to run 13 – almost double the number! This will be possible because trains will pass at Winchcombe and at Gotherington. Although this means the end of the Winchcombe shuttles, it does mean more mileage possible between Toddington and Cheltenham with very short turn-rounds at both ends of the line making a fuller day of train travel possible.

Next the whole event then needs to be publicised. There is no point running an event like this on a huge scale only to find that no one turns up because nobody knows about it. Approved adverts are placed in a handful of railway press as well as being heavily mentioned on-line, especially in forums. With visiting locos, it adds an extra appeal for potential visitors and the design of adverts needs to be carefully considered to make them eye-catching.

Attention is then turned to the rostering of locos to the timetable which by now would, hopefully, have been agreed by the Railways' Operations Department. Normal practise is

to give each loco a fair crack and balance the mileages out - this is not as easy as it may seem. Many frustrating hours later, a draft loco roster is sent round to the planning committee who then take their copy away and discuss it with their respective groups. Nine times out of ten someone will not be happy and we always try our best to accommodate any changes suggested, but sometimes this simply is not possible. There is a 'norm' where we try and keep one set with Sulzer-engined locos on and one set of stock with English Electric locos on. While this is not always possible – believe me, we do try!

Once the loco roster is pretty much complete, a copy is then sent to our roster clerks who appeal for traincrew – each locomotive requires one driver and one secondman. With our entire home fleet in operation on both days at a weekend, we require at least seven sets of crew (more if we have visiting locos) – sometimes this seems almost impossible but is always a relief when all the slots are filled – normally about a week before the event.

In addition, at an operations meeting approximately two months prior to the event, the guards department are given a copy of the timetable and asked to provide the required number of crews (normally three guards and three TTIs for our event).

The last bit of paperwork to arrange is the 'Movement Orders'. After sitting down for a few hours, each locomotive's exact move is worked out and typed up. A copy can then be printed and put in the driving cab of each of the locos so that the crews know where they are supposed to be and when – and perhaps more importantly – what their next move is. A signal box copy is also published and posted in Toddington signalbox so the signalman is aware of who goes where and when.

You cannot immediately see that when you arrive at Toddington you need to run up the headshunt and back into the Parlour Road to stable for instance, so with this information right in front of the crews, the event should run like clockwork. As we all know though, it does not – but we'll come back to that in a moment.

With all the pre-planning done, the next thing is for loco owners to check over their respective engines and make sure they are operational for the event. No one wants a loco to 'sit down' in the middle of a gala and while it is impossible to check over every single detail before the event, the locos are given a thorough service and a run-up for testing in the days prior to the event.

Fuel levels are checked (fuel delivery is normally arranged several weeks in advance to ensure the tanks are full) and water and oil levels also checked and double checked. Batteries are also put on charge if required to make sure that the loco will start – always a bonus! Anyone involved with the running of a heritage diesel will know that they can sometimes be temperamental machines.

For a loco that groups are unsure about – there's nothing like a test-run to find and sort out any problems if required. This is normally done in the week prior to the event and arranged in conjunction with the Operations Department when there are no other services working. Normally, a test run is tied in with stock movements – moving coaching sets from Winchcombe to Toddington and shunting them in the correct order for the start of service on the first day of the gala.

When the big day finally arrives, many months after the initial planning stages, all fingers are crossed in the hope that nothing will go wrong. As well as all the train crew and guards, many other staff are involved with the running of the event – stationmasters and station staff, signalmen and perhaps most importantly, the Duty Operations Officer. The running of the trains and keeping trains to time is their responsibility and is everyone's first point of contact if there is a problem. The Duty Operations Officer is rostered from the Operations department and is fully briefed on the event, having been issued with a full copy of all the paperwork (timetable, loco and crew roster, movements orders etc). Should there be a problem with a locomotive and a substitute needs to be made, or if trains start running late for any reason, only the Duty Operations Officer has the authority to amend the timetable, although this is usually done in

conjunction with a member of the planning committee who knows the event inside out.

At the end of the day, all locos are shunted around (normally by one of the latter arrivals on shed) so that they are in position for the Sunday morning departures – there is nothing worse than turning up early on a Sunday morning to 'prep' your loco only to find that another loco (or two!) are parked in the way meaning much shunting to release your motive power for the day!

On the evening of the Sunday of the event, one or two traincrew are 'volunteered' to shunt the stock into the correct order and return the third rake of carriages to Winchcombe where they will stable. Only when the last loco is back on shed safely, is the event well and truly over.

Finally, when the event is over, everyone breathes a sigh of relief and we eagerly await details of the ticket sales – the higher the passenger number the more profit the event makes meaning the Railway will happily accommodate our events for another year – that's what it all boils down to – keeping passengers happy so they return gala after gala, year after year.

The problem for the planning committee though is that they've already started the entire process all over again for the next event. ■

Top: *The signing on point for staff at Toddington depot. The locomotive crew's sheet is the one nearest the camera.* **Chris Perkins**

Top Right: *Paul Fuller processes paperwork in the office at Toddington depot in connection with a forthcoming gala.* **Chris Perkins**

Right: *Paul Fuller discusses operational matters with Gloucestershire Warwickshire Railway driver Mark Bridges in the cab of Class 37/0 No. 37215.* **Chris Perkins**

Above: *A view of the locomotive depot at Toddington. Stabled locomotives include Class 08 No. 08683, Class 73 No. 73129 which can be seen undergoing a much needed repaint from very faded Network Southeast livery into Electric Blue in the David Page shed in the background. Class 37/3 No. 37324* **Clydebridge** *and Class 24 No. 24081 are seen on the left.* Chris Perkins

Right Middle: *Paul Fuller carries out a walkround preparation of Class 47 No. 47376* **Freightliner 1995** *in the yard at Toddington shed prior to working a service from Toddington later in the day.* Chris Perkins

Right: *Having carried out the walkround inspection and removed the exhaust port covers Paul Fuller starts No. 47376* **Freightliner 1995** *prior to moving off the shed.* Chris Perkins

Above: *Because the railway is not mainline connected all visiting locomotives have to arrive and depart using road transport. Following it's visit from the East Lancs Railway Class 24 No.* D5054 **Phil Southern** *is loaded in the car park for the return home on 18 January 2009. An ex-GWR Tool Van can be seen arriving on a low loader in the background.* Paul Fuller

Below: *Gloucestershire Warwickshire Railway operated, but privately owned Class 20 No.* D8137 *is seen running nose first as it passes the fields at Didbrook with a demonstration ballast train from Toddington to Winchcombe on 6 July 2008.* Jamie Squibbs

Above: *In late afternoon sunshine on 25 October 2009, the railway's latest resident Class 37/0 No. 37248 still in West Coast Railway maroon livery following a period of hire to them and in the care of The Growler Group, approaches Hailes overbridge with the 15.10 Toddington to Cheltenham Race Course.* Mark Few

Below: *Class 73/1 No. 73129, previously named* **City of Winchester** *has just passed under Hailes overbridge on 5 November 2006 hauling the 10.42 Toddington to Winchcombe local service. 2010 was the last year the locomotive carried this livery as it was repainted into 1960s Electric Blue livery in spring 2010, a livery it first carried when delivered from Vulcan Foundry in June 1966.* Chris Perkins

Above: *During the November 2006 diesel gala Class 47 No. 47105 heads a demonstration freight from Toddington along the straight from the Hailes direction and approaches Chicken Curve heading for Winchcombe. This area can only be accessed with a lineside pass.* **Chris Perkins**

Below: *Resident Class 20 No. D8137 heads through the 10mph restriction on Chicken Curve on 5 November 2006 with the 11.15 Winchcombe to Toddington local service.* **Chris Perkins**

Above: *During the gala on 9 September 2006 the secondman of Class 37 No. 37324* **Clydebridge** *hands over the single line token to the Winchcombe signalman on the approach to the station with the 15.00 from Toddington to Cheltenham Race Course.* **Chris Perkins**

Below: *After a period in store and resident on the line for a short period, Class 47/7 No. 47701* **Waverley** *arrives at Winchcombe with the 14.00 Cheltenham Race Course to Toddington on 5 July 2008. This locomotive is now based on the Dartmoor Railway at Meldon.* **Chris Perkins**

Above: *On the Christmas diesel running day 27 December 2008, East Lancs Railway based Class 24 No. D5054* **Phil Southern** *emerges from the 693 yard long Greet tunnel and approaches Winchcombe with a morning service from Cheltenham Race Course to Toddington. The visit of this locomotive brought together two of the four preserved Class 24s on the same railway for a short period.* **Mark Few**

Below: *Class 56 No. 56003 still in Loadhaul livery was based on the railway for a time after preservation and is seen on Sunday 25 September 2005 in Dixton cutting approaching the overbridge with an afternoon Toddington to Cheltenham Race Course working. This locomotive is now part of the Hanson Traction fleet as No. 56312* **Artemis**. *It is paired with Class 73 No. 73129 as a vacuum brake translator for the Mk 1 stock.* **Chris Perkins**

Above: *A view from the cab of Class 37 No. 37215 at Gotherington showing the recent work carried out here with the new loop, signal box and signals. At the time of writing all trains were terminating here due to a substantial landslip approximately 200 yards long in the area of the bracket signal in the left distance.* Chris Perkins

Left: *During the Spring Gala in 2008 Class 27 No. 27066 visited from the Dean Forest Railway and is recorded passing Southam Lane overbridge with the 11.40 Toddington to Cheltenham Race Course.* Chris Perkins

Below: *Resident Class 20 No. D8137 and No. D8142 from the Llangollen Railway have just departed Cheltenham Race Course on 9 September 2006 with the 12.20 to Toddington and approach Southam Lane overbridge. No. D8142 is now based at Barrow Hill.* Chris Perkins

8

9

Euro Rail Hot Spots

By Philip Wormald

The photo locations in this short guide are a personal selection of busy rail 'hubs' which are in scenic areas and are popular spots found in other guides to enhance a standard railway photograph to include something of the landscape, such as a river, church or similar subject.

All of the locations in this article (with the exception of the Spanish entry) are all within walking distance of station, and a map has been included to show the basic location, further directions can easily be found 'on line' by simple typing the name of the 'hot spot' into "Google Maps" on any internet connected computer, this gives a choice of aerial or map views making studying locations extremely easily.

A dedicated Yahoo group "IRP" International Railway Photography has been set up to assist people in reporting on these and other locations.
http://groups.yahoo.com/group/International-Railway-Photography ■

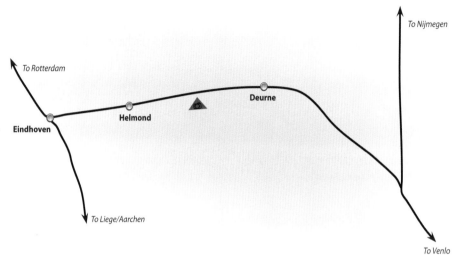

Deurne, Holland

The location Deurne, Holland is situated just west of Venlo on the line from the German border towards Den Haag. As the line is east to west it is a location where a full day can be spent.

There is a very intensive passenger service of half hourly InterCity (IC) trains between Den Haag and Venlo (nowadays around 30 per cent are worked by Class 1700s on push-pull sets), the remainder are formed of new double deck EMUs.

The local services are still worked by the classic old "dog head" EMUs which have been part of the Dutch rail scene for many years.

The location is situated a couple of kilometers west of Deurne station and with a small stream in the foreground the spot offers a lovely display of trains in the peaceful Dutch countryside. It is easily accessible by foot from Deurne station.

Traction on the freight trains is often DB Class 189s and various operators Class 66s and other private operator classes, these include, ACTS, ITL, Crossrail, ERS, HGK, TXL.

There are eight trains an hours calling at Deurne, so plenty of scope for the visitor. ■

Below: *Nederlandse Spoorwegen (NS) 1700 class No. 1776 is photographed just west of Deurne in the late afternoon of 5 August 2009 powering westbound train IC1952 from Venlo to Den Haag. The train is formed of ICR carriages in push-pull formation. Three sub classes of the 1700 class exist No. 1701-28 are InterCity locos, Nos. 1729-34 are mixed locos and Nos. 1736-1781 are push pull fitted and can operate with double deck stock.* **PW**

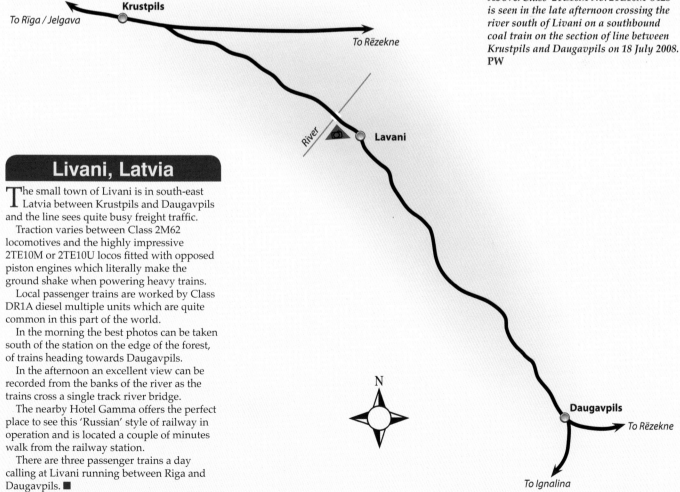

Above: Class 2TE10M No. 2TE10M-3425 is seen in the late afternoon crossing the river south of Livani on a southbound coal train on the section of line between Krustpils and Daugavpils on 18 July 2008. PW

Livani, Latvia

The small town of Livani is in south-east Latvia between Krustpils and Daugavpils and the line sees quite busy freight traffic.

Traction varies between Class 2M62 locomotives and the highly impressive 2TE10M or 2TE10U locos fitted with opposed piston engines which literally make the ground shake when powering heavy trains.

Local passenger trains are worked by Class DR1A diesel multiple units which are quite common in this part of the world.

In the morning the best photos can be taken south of the station on the edge of the forest, of trains heading towards Daugavpils.

In the afternoon an excellent view can be recorded from the banks of the river as the trains cross a single track river bridge.

The nearby Hotel Gamma offers the perfect place to see this 'Russian' style of railway in operation and is located a couple of minutes walk from the railway station.

There are three passenger trains a day calling at Livani running between Riga and Daugavpils. ∎

Wassen, Switzerland

Wassen is one of the all time classic locations in Europe, located on the busy Gotthard route in Switzerland.

The former station at Wassen is closed, but an hourly bus service operates as replacement and it is only a few minutes north of Göschenen to reach this wonderful photographic vantage point.

The classic shot of southbound trains is best in the afternoon, but with trains spiralling round three levels of tracks there is always plenty of action.

Two passenger trains an hour pass in each direction, currently a mix of SBB ICN tilting EMUs and Class Re4/4II are used.

Freight traffic can be seen powered by SBB Re4/4II and Re6/6 in multiple (known as Re10) and sometimes even an Re20!

DB Class 185s now also feature on many Gotthard trains as well as some private operator locos where power runs through from Germany and even on into Switzerland.

After a southbound train passes on the lower lever (the best place for a photo) it will reappear a minute or so later heading in the opposite direction as it heads further down the valley and will then appear again around five minutes later in the opposite direction again as it heads for the town at Göschenen.

This location has to be one of the all time best in the world for watching Swiss Railways. ∎

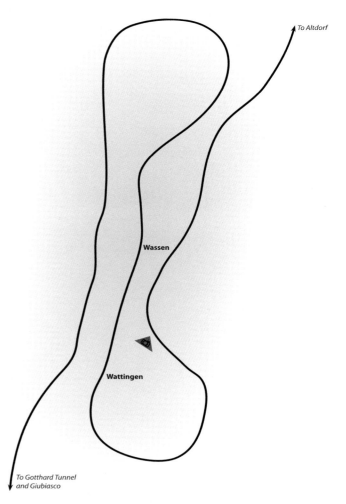

To Altdorf

Wassen

Wattingen

To Gotthard Tunnel and Giubiasco

Below: *Powered by Re 460 class No. 460.064 is seen at Wassen on 24 May 2006 forming train EC111 from Basel SBB - Venezia Santa Lucia. The train is formed of "Cisalpino" liveried Swiss carriages. 119 Re460 Bo-Bo locos frequently called Lok2000s are in operation on SBB, introduced from 1991 these locos develop 6100kW (8,180hp) and have a top speed of 230km/h (143mph). PW*

Above: 25kV ac 1500 class No. 15004 is seen crossing the River Marne shortly before Nanteuil-Sâacy, just after sunrise on 22 May 2007 powering train EC63 from Paris Est to München on 22 May 2007. The slight mist in the background enhances the picture with the near perfect reflection in the river water. This train is formed of a French locomotive and German (DB) stock. PW

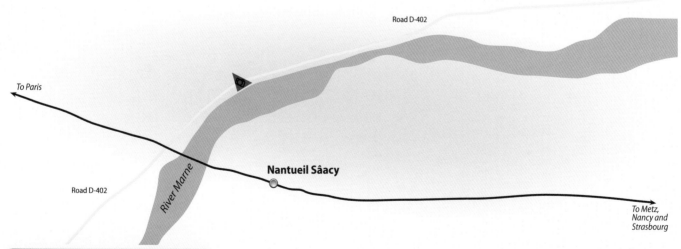

Nanteuil Sâacy, France

Nanteuil-Saacy is just 74 kilometres east of Paris on the classic line from Paris Est to Metz, Nancy and Strasbourg.

Since the introduction of TGV Est, the passenger service has been reduced but there are still some trains passing with Class 15000 electric locos on the basic two hourly service to St Dizier, Chalons en Champagne or Bar-le-Duc.

There is also a considerable amount of freight passing with mostly the Alsthom 'Prima' freight locos of Classes 27000 and 37000.

The classic photo of the train crossing the river is just after sunrise. An hourly local train service operates from Paris Est - Chateau-Thierry and trains call at Nanteuil-Sâacy. A lovely early morning photo can be taken as trains burst out of

the tunnel and cross the river from a quite spot behind a bus stop on the banks of the river.

Once the sun is off the bridge in the morning an embankment at the station allows for photos later in the day as they pass this quiet and remote town.

The Hotel Auberge du Lion d'or is located very close to the station. ∎

Above: *Railion-operated DB-Schenkar Class 185 No. 185.172 is viewed from the vantage point shown on the map at Retzbach-Zellingen on a westbound mixed wagon-load freight on 14 April 2009. The low-level lighting shows the view was recorded shortly before sunset. The Class 185s are dual voltage locos capable of operating from either 15 or 25kV ac.* PW

Retzbach-Zellingen, Germany

The photo location at Retzbach-Zellingen is situated on a bridge above the station of the same name located between Würzburg and Gemünden.

It is a busy spot as it captures much of the freight workings on the north - south München - Hamburg and the east - west Passau - Frankfurt routes.

The classic shot of a train heading west towards Gemünden is best shot in the late afternoon when hopefully the sun is shining.

There is a vast mix of traction on this line including DB Classes 101, 111, 112, 120, 140, 145, 146, 151, 152, 182, 185, 189 and a good selection of private operator locos including Voith 'Maxima' and 'Blue Tiger' locomotives.

There are hourly local trains stopping at the station and the photo spot is located above the station on the bridge, to reach the spot it is necessary to walk for about 10 minutes into town to gain access to the road going on the bridge.

Four trains an hour call at Retzbach-Zellingen, two are Regional Express (RE) trains from Frankfurt/M - Würzburg or Nürnberg and two are Regional (RB) trains most of which run on the Schlüctern - Würzburg route.

An ideal ticket to use in this area is the very good value Bayern "Lander" ticket which is valid from Karl (just south of Frankfurt/M) and covers the large Bayern region in the south of Germany. ∎

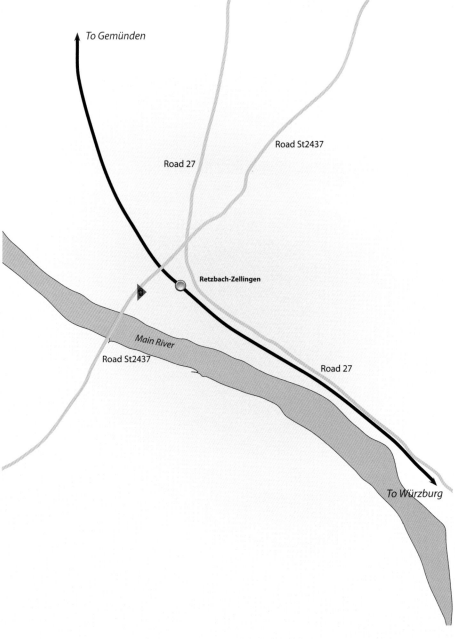

To Gemünden

Road St2437

Road 27

Retzbach-Zellingen

Main River

Road St2437

Road 27

To Würzburg

Himmelstadt, Germany

The photo location at Himmelstadt, Germany is perched high up on some cliffs around 30 minutes walk from the small station located at Himmelstadt.

The best feature of photography from this location is the ability to get a barge passing on the Main River in the background alongside a train, there are regular slow moving vessels passing on this section, so it is not as difficult as it sounds.

There is a large amount of freight activity on this busy line between Würzburg and Gemünden.

The best images are probably taken with the sun shortly after sun rise. DB locos of Classes 101, 111, 112, 120, 140, 145, 146, 151, 152, 182, 185, 189 and a good selection of private operator locos can be found on most days.

There are hourly local trains serving Himmelstadt, these are hauled by Class 111, 112 or 143 locos operating in push-pull mode. ■

Right: *As long as you have the feet of a mountain goat and don't mind heights, this has to be one of the most impressive views of a canal, railway and road anywhere. DB Cargo Class 152s Nos. 152.004 and 152.014 are seen from the cliffs at Himmelstadt powering a southbound freight on the morning of 15 April 2009. PW*

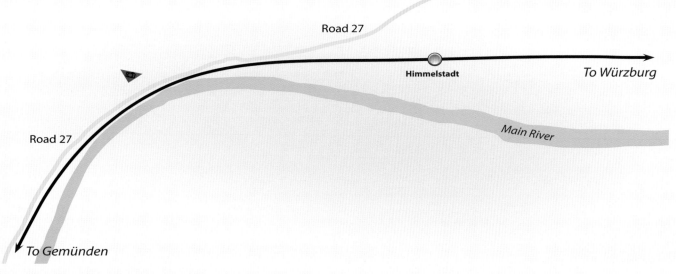

Road 27

Himmelstadt

To Würzburg

Road 27

Main River

To Gemünden

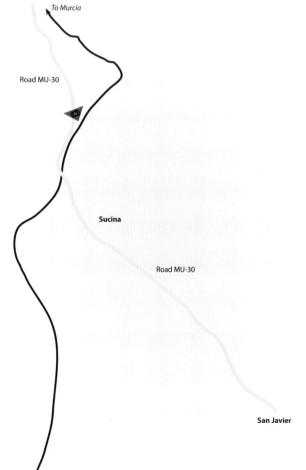

Above: *Class 333.3 No. 333.353 is seen in the morning light near Sucina on train No. 55044 conveying cement from Cementos Tajo to Escombreras on 15 November 2007. 77 Class 333.3 locos are in freight service with Renfe these were rebuilt in 2002-07 by Alstom and have a 'Prima' style body. PW*

Above: *Class 334 No. 334.012 is seen near Sucina on Talgo train 460 from Cartagena to Montpellier on 18 November 2007. The '334' works the Cartagena to Alicante section of this long distance train and the loco runs round during the reversal at Murcia del Carmen. PW*

Sucina, Spain

Sucina is a very remote location in south eastern Spain located on the non-electrified diesel line between Murcia del Carmen and Cartagena.

Road transportation is required to get to this location, but with a stunning mountainous background it is a wonderful photographic viewpoint to visit. This sort of backdrop is similar with many of the lines in the southern half of Spain.

Passenger trains from Cartagena to Madrid are hauled throughout by modern Class 334 diesels hauling rakes of Talgo stock, and at busy times these trains have double consists and can be quite long.

Local trains tend to be very small and some are even formed of single Class 596 railcars.

Freight traffic is handled by large General Motors-powered Class 333.3s belonging to the cargo sector of RENFE (the Spanish national rail operator). Around two or three freights a day normally pass this section of line. ∎

St Jodok, Austria

One of the all time classic photo locations in Europe is the large horseshoe curve high above the town of St Jodok in the idyllic Brenner Pass between Innsbruck and Brennero.

There is a large amount of freight traffic on this line and most of these trains feature either double headed locos or locos on each end of the train, sometimes three or even more locos can be seen on one train.

A large proportion of these locos are private operator traction. Currently the two hourly EuroCity trains from München to destinations in Italy are powered by FNM (Ferrovie Milano Nord) Class 189s, but these are expected to hand over to ÖBB Class 1216 in the near future.

Virtually all the local stopping trains from Innsbruck and Brennero are now in the hands of 'Talent' EMUs. The Innsbruck to Lienz corridor trains also pass this way with Class 1216 locos.

The sun is best for southbound (downhill) trains in the morning once the sun has got above the mountains. There are a couple of fields which give a great view, but be careful as one of the farmers will only tolerate visitors on the edge of his fields!

The Gasthoff Lamm hotel is situated in the middle of the town and provides a fine view of the trains from some of the rooms.

The local ÖBB 'Tirol Ticket' allows one week of unlimited travel in this beautiful part of Austria for €53. ∎

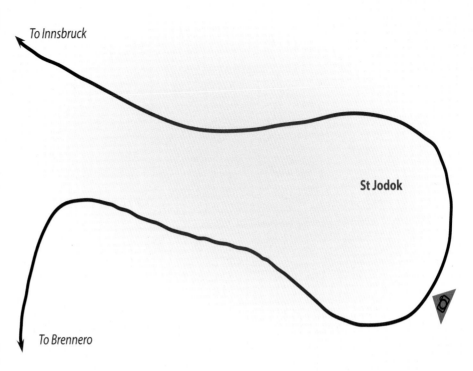

To Innsbruck

To Brennero

St Jodok

Below: *A fleet of 60 Class 1216 Bo-Bo triple voltage electrics are in operation with Österreichische Bundesbahnen (Austrian Railways). The fleet entered service from 2006 and are based on the Taurus design. No. 1216.141 is seen in the mid morning traversing the stunning Brenner pass on downhill 'RoLa' train passing St Jodok on 21 September 2006, a further 1216 class loco can be seen on the rear of the train. The truck drivers are carried in the coach behind the leading loco which provides food and rest for the drivers.* PW

The Waterloo & City Line
During the LSWR, Southern and BR era

By Colin J. Marsden

During the mid-1840s the London and South Western Railway (L&SWR) could foresee huge financial benefit from having a terminus close or within the City of London. In 1846 authorisation was given for an extension of the L&SWR line to London Bridge, but due to the financial crisis of the time, plans for the extension were abandoned in 1848.

Following the success of the City and South London Railway during the 1890s the L&SWR decided that an extension to the City of London was required and plans were drawn up by W. R. Galbraith, R. F. Church and J. N. Greathead, a firm of well-known engineers of the period, for an underground railway.

Work commenced on the line in June 1894 and was completed early in 1898. Building work was effected by J. Mowlem & Co, who carried out the tunnel boring and lining work, while Perry & Co, carried out the station construction work at Waterloo and Bank.

The route taken for the City extension of the L&SWR was from below Waterloo main line station along the course of Stamford Street, under the River Thames near Blackfriars, and then below Queen Victoria Street to Mansion House and the City station.

The up and down lines were constructed in single bore cement-lined tunnels to alleviate excessive underground noise, with a diameter of 12ft 1¾in (3.70m) increasing to 12ft 9in (3.89m) on curves.

At the terminus at Waterloo the line was around 40ft (12.2m) below rail height of the main line station, or 17ft (5.18m) below street level. As the line progressed towards the City it lowered to a level of 23ft (7m) below the bed of the River Thames and when the line reached Bank it was 59ft (18m) below street level. The maximum permitted speed for trains on the line at opening was 35mph (56km/h) on the straight track with 10-15mph (16-24km/h) restrictions on curves, after several years, the Board of Trade permitted an increase to 20mph (32km/h) on curves.

The new Waterloo & City line was officially opened by the Duke of Cambridge on 11 July 1898 but did not open to fare-paying passengers until 8 August 1898.

Rolling stock for the new line was provided in the form of five four-car trains later supplemented by five single car powered units. The four-car sets were built by Jackson and Sharp of Wilmington, USA with power equipment supplied by Siemens. The bogies at each end of a four-car train contained two 60hp (45kW) gearless motors with armatures direct on the axles. The five single power cars were built in 1899 by Dick Kerr & Co Ltd of Preston, as four-car sets were not required on the line during off peak periods.

This rolling stock remained in service until the line was modernised during 1940 and new English Electric stock built.

Power was originally supplied by the line's own steam generator located at Waterloo, but this was relegated to standby status in 1915 when the L&SWR main line electrification took place, and from then power was supplied from the main line substation. The lines live rail was energised 600V dc.

The Waterloo & City line was also the home to one locomotive used for shunting coal wagons from the hydraulic lift siding to the power generating station, and was occasionally used for depot shunting and some permanent way work. The locomotive was a 'Bo' electric of 1898 built by Siemens, and can now be viewed as part of the National Railway Museum collection at York.

The signalling system for the line was originally Sykes 'lock and block', designed by the signal engineer Mr W. R. Sykes, who together with Mr J. P. Annett was greatly involved with the design of a novel signal system on the line. Semaphore signals could be used at the stations but an alternative method had to be developed for the tunnel sections, due to the limited clearances. For this, Sykes developed a colour-light system worked by an electro-magnet which moved a red or green lens across a bulb, and so gave a signal to the driver; lamp proving was provided in the signalboxes which were situated at each end of the line. A very early form of automatic train control (ATC) was provided by means of a 'slapper-bar', which was a length of insulated rail placed on the side of the track at a signal, and which was charged with low voltage current when the signal was 'on' (at danger); a small arm on the train's side slid along this rail and energised a release coil which in turn tripped the main power switch of the train. This very basic equipment worked with few failures until 1940 when the line was equipped under the modernisation plan with track circuits, colour-light signalling, and electro-pneumatic train stops (of a type used on the London Transport lines). From then, the signal box at Waterloo controlled all signals and points at Waterloo together with signals in the tunnels. At Bank an automatic pre-select panel was installed to operate signals and points. This equipment was capable of automatically running trains to/from alternate platforms during peak periods, and using only one platform during off peak times. If an emergency arose the panel could be worked manually.

Also installed under the rebuilding was a system of 'pinch wires', which were two bare copper wires running along each tunnel wall at cab window height. If a driver required to talk with the signalman due to a failure or emergency, he could clip a telephone hand set on to the wires; as well as giving communication with the signalman at Waterloo, this would turn on the tunnel lights, discharge the live rail supply and give the driver/signalman telephonic communication with the power supply controller at Raynes Park, who was responsible for the power to the Waterloo and City line.

During the 1940 rebuilding new stock was designed and built. 12 motor coaches and 16 trailers were constructed by English Electric at the Dick Kerr Works in Preston - the same works that had built the five single power cars in 1899. The new stock was of welded steel construction and was far more comfortable and cleaner than the original US-built vehicles. The new motor coaches were powered by two 190hp axle-hung traction motors, situated at one end of the power car (the Bank end). Driving cabs were fitted with a standard English Electric four position power controller at each end, together with a Westinghouse direct air brake system of identical design to that fitted to the current suburban units on the main line.

Behind the driving position at the motor bogie end was an equipment room, housing the main equipment fuse, line switches, reversers, power contractors, motor isolating switches, overload and current limit relays, control and compressor governor, control cut out switch, emergency lighting battery and emergency tools.

Mounted on the underframe were the main power resistances and air compressor. The total weight of a motor coach was 23tons and each could seat 40, with room for a further 60 standing. Trailer cars were of similar body construction and weighed just 19tons, seating 52 with standing room for 80.

When built, the rolling stock was painted in Southern Railway green, but during the 1970s BR standard rail blue was applied. Trains were normally formed into five-car sets - a power car at each end with three trailers between. During off peak periods single power cars could be operated, but in normal operating practice two power cars are coupled together, following brake problems with single vehicles.

Routine maintenance of rolling stock was carried out at the line's own workshops at Waterloo, this was equipped with all major workshop items. Body lifting for bogie removal could also be accommodated. For classified or specialised repair rolling stock was removed from the line by means of an Armstrong

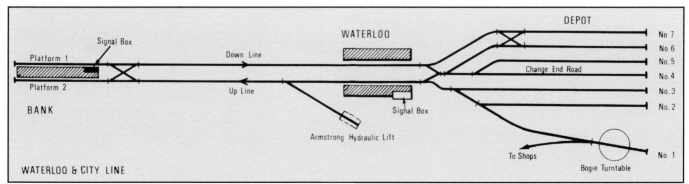

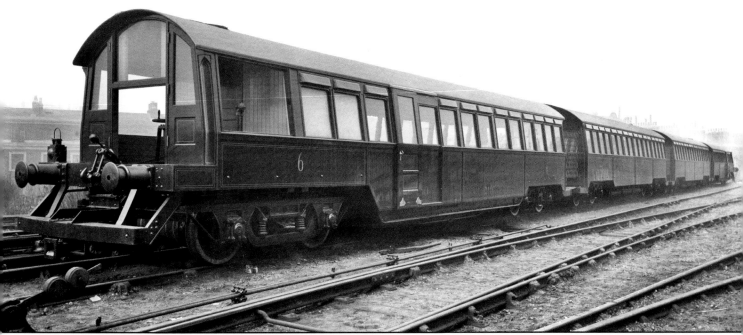

Above: *A very rare illustration of the original Waterloo & City stock, showing a complete four-car train of 1898 built Jackson & Sharp stock, parked in sidings at Waterloo before lowering onto the line. The lattice gates can clearly be seen between the cars. It is interesting to note that this stock has more conventional draw gear and a centre hook and shackle coupler. This train later formed train 'C' on the line and was formed of cars 6, 27, 28, 29 and 12.* **CJM Collection**

hydraulic lift platform with a maximum load capacity of 30tons, this was located on a spur near the Waterloo end of the 'up' line. The hydraulic platform reached main line level in the north sidings of the main line station.

Originally the lift was used a great deal when coal and engineering wagons were lowered to the line on a daily basis, but in later years it was only rarely used. When stock was required to travel on the lift, very precise loading had to take place as even with couplings removed there was only two/three inches (5-8cm) to spare.

When stock was required for heavy repair Selhurst depot usually undertook this work, but from the late 1970s Stewarts Lane and East Wimbledon depots commenced bogie repair work.

Drivers for the Waterloo and City line were taken from the links of men at Waterloo main line depot, while guards were employed solely for W&C rosters and were not trained on any

Below: *A pair of 1940-built English Electric Dick Kerr DMB vehicles Nos. S62 and S51 are seen at platform one of Bank station on 26 August 1981. In off-peak periods and depending on maintenance requirements of the trailer vehicles it was not uncommon to find two power cars working without trailer stock, this gave for some lively running and speeds well in excess of 35mph were recorded on a number of occasions. It was possible for a single DMB to operate alone, but this practice ceased in the 1960s after a near runaway.* **Colin J. Marsden**

Above: One of the most amazing Southern electric workings to ever be recorded took place in September 1977 when Waterloo & City DMB No. S58 was removed from the isolated line and transferred by rail between barrier wagons to Farnham depot. Between 26-28 September 1977 the vehicle operated during the off-peak period between Farnham and Alton under its own power for speedometer development work and testing of other equipment. Devoid of any yellow end, marker lights or even a windscreen wiper No. S58 worked well and made some SR EMU history. The car is seen departing from Farnham on 27 February 1977 as the 10.04 to Alton. Colin J. Marsden

Below: The depot at Waterloo was very cramped with just enough space for all sets to be stabled at night. During the day to facilitate maintenance a number of shunt moves had to be undertaken and for this purpose one of the drivers duties was maintained for depot shunting. DMB cars S57 (left) and S61 (right) stand side by side in the maintenance lines at Waterloo depot on 15 May 1981. Colin J. Marsden

Above: Under the days of Network SouthEast, the Waterloo & City line was cleaned up with platforms improved, and trains repainted in the NSE red, white and blue colours, sporting both BR double arrow and NSE branding. With its arbatory red lights desplayed on both front and rear, a five car formation led by car No. S57 awaits to depart from Waterloo to Bank on 28 May 1993, the final day of operation for the 1940 built stock. Colin J. Marsden

Right Middle: The interior of the Class 487 or 1940s built stock was very cramped, with longitudinal seating at vehicle ends and groups of four facing seats either side of a narrow central corridor in the middle of coaches. One end of each DMB vehicle had a raised floor to allow space for the power bogie. This view shows the interior of a TS vehicle in the later Network SouthEast days with NSE blue moquette and bodyside advertising. Colin J. Marsden

Right Bottom: The interior of Waterloo (Waterloo & City Line) signal box. This had a 16 lever frame and controlled the complex crossing arrangement at Waterloo and running signals. The point work in the yard was manual and operated by depot shunting staff. The box shelf showed detection for points and signals and housed two block bells - one for the 'up' and one for the 'down' line. This view was recorded im May 1981. Colin J. Marsden

1940 stock technical data

	DMBS	TS
Class No.:	487	487
Car Nos.:	S51-S62	S71-S86
Introduced:	1940	1940
Weight:	23 ton	19 ton
Length:	49ft 1¾in (14.98m)	49ft 1¾in (14.98m)
Height:	9ft 7in (2.92m)	9ft 7in (2.92m)
Width:	8ft 7¾in (2.63m)	8ft 7¾in (2.63m)
Brake type:	Auto-air	Auto-air
Traction Motor:	2 x EE500	-
Car power:	380hp (283.3kW)	-
Gear ratio:	69:16	-
Max Speed:	35mph (56km/h)	35mph (56km/h)
Seating car:	40 second	52 second
Seating train:	2-car - 80 second	
	5-car - 236 second	

other types of stock.

In the 1970s, the service on the line was based on a four train working method during the peak hours with trains formed of five cars giving a total passenger loading of 596.

Services commenced from Waterloo at 06.46 on Monday to Friday and 06.45 on Saturday, while the first train from Bank departed at 06.45 on Monday to Friday and 06.51 on Saturday. The last services of the day departed from Waterloo at 21.45 on Monday to Friday, and 13.52 on Saturday; final departures from Bank were 22.02 Monday to Friday, and 13.59 on Saturday. The line had no Sunday service .

Another unique feature of the Waterloo & City line is the Travolater at Bank station. When opened on 27 September 1960, this was the first of its type in Europe. The Travolater is a twin parallel travelling 'pavement', each being 302ft 6in (92.2m) long rising at an angle of 8 deg. The speed was normally 2.04mph, but this was adjustable dependent upon the number of passengers being carried. Each pavement

was formed of 488 40in x 16in (1.01m x 0.4m) steel decks carried on four ball bearing wheels. Normally one pavement worked in each direction, but during peak periods both were often set to operate in the same direction, giving an hourly passenger flow rate of 16,200.

Following the formation of Network SouthEast as a separate business unit of BR controlling London area and suburban services from 1986, the Managing Director Chris Green immediately set out a modernisation plan for the Waterloo & City line, this at first saw the 1940s built trains repainted from rail blue into NSE red white and blue livery and considerable station improvement work carried out.

The depot at Waterloo was considerably modernised with a separate workshop formed, including new overhead cranes which were able to carry out a much improved maintenance of stock.

By the early years of the 1990s, new stock was sought for the line, this was a considerable challenge for NSE engineers. Eventually a

follow-on order for London Underground Central Line stock was authorised in 1991, with 10 two-car train sets built by ABB/Adtranz Derby and delivered in 1993.

Concurrent with the delivery of this stock, the Waterloo & City line was closed for several months for total refurbishment, this included track replacement, alterations to the sidings at Waterloo and the building of a new access opening on the south side of Waterloo main line station to remove and lower stock to the line, this was required as the original hydraulic lift in Waterloo north sidings had been removed as part of the new Waterloo International station.

The 1993 modernisation saw the removal of all remaining 1940 BR stock (classified as 487 under TOPS).

The Waterloo & City line operated with the new stock - classified as Class 482 - between July 1993 and 1 April 1994 when the line was transferred to London Underground control, this was deemed the best option with privatisation of the UK rail system from 1996. ∎

Waterloo and City

Left: *One of the most momentous occasions in the history of Waterloo came in 1993 when the Waterloo & City line was modernised and the 1940s stock removed from the railway to be replaced by pure London Underground vehicles. As part of the 1993 line improvement package a new opening was made to the Waterloo & City line, as the original lift on the north side of the main line station had been removed as part of the construction of the International terminal. The new opening was not rail connected on the surface and all vehicles being removed and delivered to the line had to arrive at Waterloo by road. These were then craned via a very tight opening onto the line using a massive road crane which required many roads around the London terminal to be closed over two separate weekends. Over the weekend of 29-30 May 1993 the first of the 1940-built cars were removed from the line and half the new fleet lowered into position. In this view we see car S59 slowly lifted out from the line, prior to being swung around over several rooftops to an awaiting road trailer parked roughly where the photographer was standing. This was a very time consuming operation with each old vehicle taking around two hours to remove from the line.*
Colin J. Marsden

Below: *With DM No. S60 nearest the camera one of the final evening departures from Bank to Waterloo arrives at Waterloo on the last day of 1940 stock operation on 28 May 1993.* Colin J. Marsden

Top: *The lowering in of the new 1993 stock was a very difficult and precise operation. A special frame was built to equal out the lifting weight and roller guides were attached to the front end which engaged in a steel channel to guide the vehicles down through the small opening and onto the track below. Car No. 67508 is seen being slowly lowered onto the line on 29 May 1993. Colin J. Marsden*

Above: *The original London & South Western electric shunting loco No. S75, later renumbered to DS75 is seen in later BR green livery in the depot at Waterloo in 1971 following a repaint and prior to removal from the line for preservation, firstly at Brighton and now as part of the National Collection at York. Colin J. Marsden*

Left: *The old Armstrong Lift, located in the North Sidings of Waterloo main line station was a fascinating piece of equipment, and one the author witnessed being used on many occasions. In this 14 October 1977 view one of the trailer vehicles is seen arriving at the surface and its slow journey from the Waterloo & City line. To reach the surface, a vehicle was hauled from the depot and pushed back into the lift spur soon after the morning peak period, then under the watchful eye of the CM&EE staff the coach was raised to the surface a trip which took around 25 minutes. Colin J. Marsden*

Above: The new 1993 Waterloo & City line stock was built as a follow-on order to the London Underground Central Line stock and was constructed by ABB/Adtranz at Derby Litchurch Lane. After testing at Derby, the sets were delivered to Ruislip LUL depot and then roaded to Waterloo for lowering onto the line. Painted in NSE livery, sets Nos. 482503 and 482504 pose on the Derby test track on 4 February 1993. Colin J. Marsden

Below: Old meets new at Waterloo depot on 28 May 1993. It was only possible to see the 1940 and 1993 stock side by side on the Waterloo and City railway for one week in mid May 1993, during the transition period from old to new stock. In this rare view taken inside Waterloo depot, we see uncommissioned 1993 set No. 482502 alongside 1940 DMB No. S59. As will be seen in this view, a considerable part of the 1990s Waterloo & City modernisation surrounded the depot at Waterloo where new overhead cranes, better illuminated pits and other safety systems were installed. Colin J. Marsden

Diesel-Hydraulic Interlude

Above: *Without doubt some of the most popular diesel locomotives of all time were the diesel-hydraulic fleets of Class 22, 35, 41, 42, 43 and 52 used on the Western Region from the early 1960s until the mid-1970s. On 14 July 1974, 'Western' No. D1043* **Western Duke** *passes Harford near Ivybridge in Devon powering train 1A45, the 12.40 Penzance to Paddington, formed of 11 Mk1 and 2 coaches.* **Bernard Mills**

Below: *With no less than three tail lights on the rear, maroon-liveried 'Western' No. D1010* **Western Campaigner** *is hauled through Exeter St Davids on 14 August 1966 by a green-liveried 'Warship'. It appears that the 'Western' was being shunted from the 'down' side to the 'up' side to be placed on Exeter depot.* **Bernard Mills**

Above: The iconic Royal Albert Bridge, designed and built by Isambard Kingdom Brunel to link the Great Western Railway between Devon and Cornwall, is probably the best known railway structure in the West Country and is still in use today, providing the sole rail connection between Devon and Cornwall. In 2010, Network Rail announced a major refurbishment of the structure, including a full repaint. On 2 October 1969, train 1C30, the 08.30 Paddington to Penzance pulls over the Royal Albert Bridge powered by 'Warship' No. D823 **Hermes** *and 'Western' No. D1011* **Western Thunderer**. *Bernard Mills*

Below: Under the modernisation plan of the Western Region, two batches of 'Warship' 2,200hp locos were built, Nos. D800-D832/D866-D870 were built by BR at Swindon, while Nos. D833-D865 were constructed by the North British Locomotive Co in Glasgow. One of the North British batch, No. D853 **Thruster** *is recorded on 28 December 1970, after some overnight snow, cresting the summit at Hemerdon, east of Plymouth with a London bound service. A goods loop exists at Hemerdon, which is still in use on the 'up' line today in which freight trains are frequently recessed to allow passenger services to overtake. Bernard Mills*

Above: *With the lower quadrant arms removed from the 'down' bracket signal on the approach to South Brent, and the trackbed of the closed Kingsbridge branch veering off to the right in the distance. 'Western' No. D1043 Western Duke approaches the closed South Brent station on 20 July 1974 while in charge of the 11.30 Paddington to Penzance service 1B45. This locomotive was withdrawn at Laira (Plymouth) in April 1976 and broken up at BREL Swindon in February 1977.* **Bernard Mills**

Left Middle: *The platelayer in this view at Saltash, appears to be looking with intrigue at a pile of wooden chair keys - perhaps he was not sure where they had come from. In the 'up' platform is rail-blue liveried Class 43 No. D843 Sharpshooter, running light loco.* **Bernard Mills**

Left Bottom: *Storming through Exminster, 'Western' No. D1046 Western Marquis heads a 12-car formation as service 1A75, the 14.40 Penzance to Paddington on 10 June 1972. This image was recorded from the Gissons farm bridge, which is still available for photography today. In the far background is the site of the closed Exminster station, which retained loops on both the 'up' and 'down' side until the mid-1980s.* **Bernard Mills**

Above: *One of the hot spots for rail activity in the diesel hydraulic era was Newton Abbot, where a sizeable depot, workshop and carriage sidings existed adjacent to the four platform station, which was a hive of activity. This is a view of the station area with the depot and works on the right, taken from a bridge at the west end, and shows 'Western' No. D1012* **Western Firebrand** *in pristine condition leading train 1C60, the 14.30 Paddington to Penzance on 28 April 1971. Today Newton Abbot is just a shadow of its former self, with only three platforms and no sidings.* **Bernard Mills**

Below: *Following the demise of four character route indicators carried by trains, most of the 'Westerns' had the route display set to show their running number, as displayed on No. D1041. On 3 July 1976, the loco passes the 'up' signal gantry at Exeter West, while heading for Plymouth with a rake of blue and grey-liveried Mk2 stock. In the background, in Exeter St Davids station a Class 33 can be seen on a Waterloo service.* **Bernard Mills**

Above: The 101-strong fleet of Beyer Peacock 'Hymek' locos were very popular with staff and had a good turn of speed when needed, especially on the Worcester-London route in the 1960s-70s. In later years carrying BR rail blue livery, the 'Hymek' fleet became staple power on the Cardiff-Bristol-Portsmouth route. On 29 April 1970, No. D7068 passes the rear of Salisbury Tunnel Junction signal box and takes the Romsey line while in charge of the 12.35 Cardiff General to Portsmouth Harbour. Bernard Mills

Below: Although the Great Western line to Hemyock closed to passenger traffic in September 1963, milk traffic continued to use the branch from Tiverton Junction until October 1975. In this view recorded on 19 April 1969, rail-blue liveried Class 22 North British Type 2 No. D6333 awaits to depart with milk tanks to Tiverton. In the background much of the original station is still seen in existence. Bernard Mills

Above: *When the Class 42 'Warship' locos were allocated to Newton Abbot, it was not uncommon to find class members powering the Exeter to Paignton stopping services, usually formed of four Mk1 coaches. Pulling away from its Dawlish stop in May 1969, No. D804* **Avenger** *heads towards Kennaway Tunnel with a late afternoon service bound for Paignton. This view has not changed a lot over the years, the viewpoint is still possible from the footpath from Teignmouth Hill through Lea Mount gardens.* **Bernard Mills**

Below: *Just west of Plymouth the Great Western main line skirted Devonport Dockyard on its way to the crossing of the River Tamar at Saltash. In this 20 March 1974 view a 'down' inter-regional service heads to Penzance powered by No. D1037* **Western Empress** *as it crosses Keyham Viaduct and past the local rugby ground. In the background are the remains of Ford Viaduct on the former Southern Railway route into Plymouth.* **Bernard Mills**

Diesels in Fenland

30 Years of Train Watching in the Cambridgeshire Fens
By Michael J. Collins, BA, Dip Ed, Cert Ed.

The Fens of East Anglia are unique – they consist of miles and miles of flat reclaimed marshland with rich black peaty soils, some of it below sea level, but all of it needing careful management by the use of Fenland drains.

Geographically the Fens stretch from just south of Cambridge sweeping northwards to The Wash and from King's Lynn westwards to Peterborough. For reasons of brevity this article will focus primarily on the Fenland district of Cambridgeshire. This region of big broad skies, is famous for its agriculture and wildlife and the area certainly contrasts greatly with the popular northern fells depicted in *Modern Locomotives Illustrated Annual No. 1*.

I firmly believe that its attractions, although different from the remote northern inclines, have been sadly under-rated by many rail enthusiasts and offers many opportunities for creative railway photography.

In railway terms my first acquaintance with the East Anglian Fens occurred in 1955 during a long journey from my native West Yorkshire to my maternal grandfather's home near Norwich. Accompanied by my late mother we had caught the York-Lowestoft through train from Doncaster and travelled by way of Lincoln and the GN/GE Joint Line to March and then onwards to Norwich via Ely.

I can even remember noting the locomotive which had pulled us over that Fenland journey - it was 'Sandringham' class 4-6-0 No. 61643 *Champion Lodge*. It was this journey and the sight of this locomotive which was the catalyst

for a lifetime of interest in trains and railways. Little did I realise on that initial acquaintance with the Fens all those years ago, that the bulk of my adult life was destined to be spent within easy reach of the area and that I would be watching and photographing trains in the Fens for well over 30 years.

March and Whitemoor

To this day the focus of much of the railway activity in the Fens is the Cambridgeshire town of March. When I first visited during 1976 the vast marshalling yard at Whitemoor was then still busy and was a major employer of the town's men. Built in the 1920s and 30s the yard was once the second largest in Europe and grew to be the largest in Britain. Even in 1975 it was still handling vast amounts of freight although the veritable river of coal trains formerly marshalled there for onward transit to London and the south had dwindled to just a trickle.

Although the gradual run-down of the yard began in the 1960s other freight remained buoyant with flows entering the yard from the north via the Great Northern/Great Eastern (GN/GE) Joint Line and from the Peterborough direction for sorting and forming trains to Temple Mills, London and to East Anglia.

The vantage point at Norwood Road bridge was a great place to observe and photograph trains with the Class 08 shunters bustling backwards and forwards assembling trains, freights entering the yard from the south and locomotives entering and departing the nearby motive power depot.

In contrast to years gone by in the steam era, when coal trains were sometimes held at every block signal between March and Temple Mills, a small amount of coal traffic remained with coal trains serving Temple Mills and one or two industrial plants in the East Anglia area. Meanwhile, the GN/GE Joint line (which bisected Whitemoor Yard) still had a passenger service and dmus forming workings to Doncaster via Lincoln were interspersed with the odd locomotive hauled extra working such as the Saturdays only/Summer Dated services connecting Great Yarmouth with Newcastle. These were booked to change engines within the Whitemoor Yard complex adjacent to Grassmoor box.

Freight to East Anglia – Transition to Speedlink – The present scene

By the mid-1970s the trains of vacuum braked freight were becoming uneconomic and the 'Speedlink' Network was developed. Wagonload freight was taken around the country from yard to yard under this system in trunk hauls. March Whitemoor was a key hub in this system and received overnight freights from most parts of the country. From March the trunk hauls would be split into smaller trip freights and were taken all around East Anglia to their ultimate destinations at places like King's Lynn, Cambridge, Parkeston Quay and various industrial concerns such as the Ciba-Geigy plant at Duxford. Other industrial plants such as the Barrington Cement Works at Foxton received deliveries from time to time.

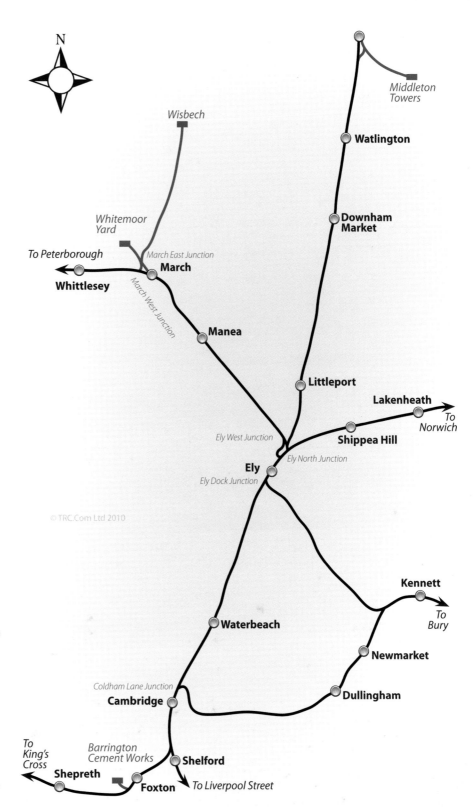

Left: Powered by Freightliner Class 66/5 No. 66568, allocated to the Intermodal pool, the 4E55 from Felixstowe to Doncaster is seen at Manea between Ely and March on 11 May 2009. MJC

Meanwhile, various stone terminals were built in East Anglia using Section 8 grants from the Government. These attracted flows of stone through East Anglia emanating from the vast stone quarries at Mountsorrel, Leicestershire. These continue to attract freight in the present day having also been joined by other stone producing outlets as far away as Stud Farm near Coalville and Peak Forest or Dowlow in Derbyshire.

A niche market also still exists in the form of a pure industrial sand product used in the Yorkshire glass making industry which is extracted from Middleton Towers, near King's Lynn. This material produces several train loads a week and is sent to Barnby Dunn and Goole.

Sadly, unlike the stone traffic which is still burgeoning, the 'Speedlink' service went into terminal decline and was axed completely soon after freight services were privatised. Whitemoor Yard was closed completely and now houses a prison complex on part of the land. More encouragingly another part of the site has more recently been converted into a hub for railway engineering services and attracts a fair amount of traffic. Soon after the closure of Whitemoor for wagonload traffic, the various industrial concerns in East Anglia which had previously generated much rail traffic, finally lost faith with moving their products in this way and have moved to using the road network.

Passenger Traffic

In the 1980s most of the long distance passenger trains were operated by locomotives and coaches. The core traffic across the Fens was the Norwich to Birmingham service (avoiding Ely by using the avoiding curve).

Below: Hauling a rake of WBB Minerals four-wheel hoppers, DBS Class 66/0 No. 66181 leads the Middleton Towers to Barnby Dunn sand train on 1 July 2008. The train is seen crossing Beggers Bridge over the Twenty Foot Drain near Whittlesey. MJC

Left: In the days prior to rail privatisation when the freight sector 'Speedlink' wagon-load network was operating, rail-blue Class 37 No. 37066 departs from the Ciba-Geigy private siding at Duxford bound for Tyne Yard on 15 August 1989. MJC

This was supplanted by passenger flows between Cambridge and Birmingham (with some services to Blackpool) and a daily service between Harwich Parkeston Quay and Manchester (later Glasgow). A daily return service between Wolverhampton and Harwich Parkeston Quay also ran.

On summer Saturdays the Fens were graced with a procession of through trains to Great Yarmouth from various Midlands and Northern cities such as Newcastle and Manchester. Sadly these have now been swept away. The Fenland town of King's Lynn had a two hourly service to London Liverpool Street which was locomotive hauled until electrification. Today, the vast majority of passenger trains across the Fens are handled by diesel or electric units. The area is popular with 'Railtour' operators, however, and continues to see visits from a number of providers. This is likely to increase with the opening, in Norfolk, of the new railway level crossing at Sheringham which allows through

running onto the North Norfolk Railway to Holt which will attract tours from all over the nation.

Parcels and Mail

During the 1980s the sight of parcels traffic was a daily occurrence in Fenland. Travelling Post Office (TPO) Mail trains connecting Liverpool Street via Ipswich to Peterborough ran in each direction at night and a number of parcels trains also traversed the area. The old Cambridge Diesel Depot, which had lain almost out of use for many years, was converted during the 1980s into a specialist depot to maintain locomotives and rolling stock used on this traffic. Empty trains used to return to this depot across the Fens from Peterborough for maintenance during the day before picking up their duties again back at Peterborough later in the evening. Sadly, railway privatisation saw the end of such traffic which was judged to be uneconomic and long trains of vans crossing the Fens are part of yesterdays railway.

Conclusion

While there is no doubt that the Fenland railway scene is not as rich in variety as it was in former days, it still has much to offer the visiting enthusiast. Passenger traffic is busier now as it has ever been (albeit in the form of diesel or electric units). Freight traffic still maintains good volumes - a total of 13 or so freights in daylight hours is not uncommon. The Fact File on the following page is a table of freights which passed Whittlesea in 24 hours on 14 January 2010.

The flat Fenland landscape can be challenging for photographers but the quality of light and superb skies compensate for it. Come on over - give it a try - you will be made very welcome. ∎

● We are aware that the spelling of 'Whittlesey' is contentious! For the purposes of this article we have used the spelling on the station name boards *not* 'Whittlesea'.

Left: With two wonderful upper-quadrant semaphore signal gantries in the view, BR red stripe grey-liveried Class 47/3 No. 47367 passes Ely North Junction on 14 May 1988. The blue and grey and Network SouthEast-liveried stock is forming a diverted King's Lynn to London Liverpool Street service, which on this day was routed to London King's Cross. MJC

Locomotive Hauled Trains at Whittlesey 14 January 2010

Passing Time	Loco	Headcode	Service
01.42	66502	4E65	22.52 Tilbury Container Terminal–Leeds Freightliner Terminal
01.54	66034	6E04	01.34 March Whitemoor–Doncaster Up Decoy
02.16	66155	6L31	02.04 Peterborough Yard–Middleton Towers WBB Minerals
02.18	66197	4E45	22.18 Felixstowe Dock DBS Siding–Wakefield Europort
02.49	66722	4L35	22.59 Doncaster Railport–Felixstowe GBRF
03.01	66559	4E03	00.27 Felixstowe North Freightliner Terminal–Doncaster Railport
04.45	66705	4E78	01.52 Felixstowe GBRF–Selby Potter Group
05.16	66566	4L83	02.31 Leeds Freightliner Terminal–Felixstowe North Freightliner Terminal
06.12	66709	6M77	05.52 March Whitemoor–Mountsorrel
06.39	66531	4L42	04.03 Doncaster Railport–Felixstowe North Freightliner Terminal
08.00	66078	6L69	07.37 Peterborough Yards–Bow Depot
09.02	66103	6M28	01.25 Ipswich West Bank Terminal–Burton on Trent
09.57	66568	4E22	05.41 Felixstowe North Freightliner Terminal–Leeds Freightliner Terminal
10.53	66155	6E84	08.20 Middleton Towers WBB Minerals–Monk Bretton
12.08	66160	6L39	09.25 Mountsorrel–Trowse, Norwich
12.12	66709	6L24	10.27 Mountsorrel–March Whitemoor
12.48	66515	6M14	10.41 Harlow Mill–Bardon Hill Quarry
14.28	66722	4E33	11.00 Felixstowe GBRF–Doncaster Railport
15.11	66078	4E25	11.25 Bow Depot–Heck (Plasmor)
16.48	66705	4L78	11.43 Selby Potter Group–Felixstowe North GBRF
17.43	66502	4L87	11.18 Leeds Freightliner Terminal–Felixstowe North Freightliner Terminal
18.27	66531	4E55	14.48 Felixstowe North Freightliner Terminal–Doncaster Railport
19.59	66016	4L45	15.25 Doncaster Decoy Up Yard–Felixstowe Dock DBS Sidings
20.32	66588	4E50	16.49 Felixstowe North Freightliner Terminal–Leeds Freightliner Terminal
20.34	66020	6L32	16.32 Burton on Trent–Ipswich West Bank Terminal
22.13	66563	4E60	18.59 Felixstowe North Freightliner Terminal–Wilton Freightliner Terminal
22.30	66502	4L79	15.45 Wilton Freightliner Terminal–Felixstowe North Freightliner Terminal
22.47	66954	4L63	19.58 Leeds Freightliner Terminal–Tilbury Container Terminal
23.08	66103	7M15	22.45 March Whitemoor–Toton Yard
23.25	66160	6M43	21.53 Trowse, Norwich–Mountsorrel

Locomotive Hauled Trains passing Whittlesey on 14 January 2010.

Below: The long distance cross-country services from East Anglia travelling via the fens always attracted the interest of haulage followers and photographers Powered by rail-blue Class 31/4 No. 31420, the 07.50 Great Yarmouth to Liverpool Lime Street is seen traversing the Ely avoiding line on 20 June 1987. MJC

Left: *With the Great Ouse in the foreground, this was the tranquil scene recorded near Ely on 14 January 1989. The full Network SouthEast-liveried train of nine Mk2s powered by like liveried Class 47 No. 47581 Great Eastern is forming the 13.00 King's Lynn to London Liverpool Street. Today the equivalent train is formed of a Class 365 and operated to and from London King's Cross.* MJC

Left Below: *Today the standard diesel locomotive motive power for the Fenland area is the Class 66. On 23 May 2007 EWS now DBS No. 66082 powers one of the daily Mountsorrel (Leicestershire) to Kennet stone trains, formed of four-wheel PGA type hoppers. The train is seen near Manea.* MJC

Below: *Carrying EWS branded Loadhaul black and orange livery, Class 60 No. 60007 passes Bield Drove near Ely in January 2008 powering the Ely Potter Group sidings to Peak Forest empty aggregate hopper service.* MJC

Right: *Superbly framed with leafless winter tree, Freightliner Class 66/5 No. 66549 powers a Barham to Dowlow aggregate train past Cow Common, Manea on 6 February 2008.* MJC

Below: *On the single line from Ely Dock Junction towards Bury, Freightliner Intermodal No. 66568 passes Leonards Crossing near Soham on 13 May 2008 while in charge of the Leeds to Felixstowe container service. Ely Cathedral can be seen to the left of the train.* MJC

Below Right: *The short lived era of Advenza Freight operating Class 66s on freight services is represented by No. 66841, the original 66406 powering the Sheerness (Kent) to Stockton scrap metal train via March on 31 July 2009. The picture was captured near Manea. This locomotive after being returned to owners Porterbrook following the demise of Advenza Freight and Cotswold Rail was subsequently re-leased to Colas Rail.* MJC

Cornish China Clay

By Cornish rail expert and historian
John A. M. Vaughan

The history of the china clay industry in Cornwall has been written about many times, suffice to say that china clay and china stone has been produced in the county for over 200 years. Once metalliferous mining activities, including tin, copper, lead and iron ore, declined in the last decades of the Victorian age the production of china clay became Cornwall's main extractive industry employing many thousands of workers.

By 1829 china clay was being carried by rail in small horse drawn wagons between St Austell and the tiny harbour of Pentewan. A complete network of railway lines gradually developed with in some cases dedicated branch lines being built to serve the industry. Clay kilns, often referred to as clay 'dries', were mostly built adjacent to railway lines, or at the end of short

Top: The current CDA circuit train is so long that the rake of wagons must be split at certain locations. On arrival at Parkandillack on a sunny October afternoon in 2007, the first 15 wagons of a rake of inbound empties have been 'cut-off' and No. 66019 runs around the first half of its train before positioning the wagons next to the loader. The remaining CDAs will later be dealt with in the same way. After loading the china clay, the train will be reformed with 38 wagons leaving the works for Carne Point. It is hard to believe that behind the visible stop blocks the line once continued to St Dennis Junction. JAMV

Left: After years of china clay train haulage by British Rail, Cornish Railways, Railfreight and Transrail a radical change occurred in the late 1990s when, on 21 October 1996, operations on a by then privatised railway found English Welsh & Scottish Railways (EWS) as the Freight Operating Company. The primary motive power in Cornwall for nearly two decades had been Class 37s, which were mostly painted in Railfreight triple grey livery. This situation remained unchanged for some time, but EWS ensured that one of the class was painted in its own colours for launch day. Their candidate was No. 37668 which looked resplendent in EW&S livery as it curved into Par station with empty CDA wagons from Carne Point to Trelavour on the Drinnick Mill branch. JAMV

Above: EWS inherited a mixture of ex-BR motive power, most of which was at least 30 years old. In Cornwall the company persevered with the Class 37s, which although reliable by reputation, were getting somewhat long in the tooth. Also to meet future EWS operational plans they were underpowered. Many of the EWS Class 37s used in Cornwall were never repainted in company colours and here a tired-looking triple grey No. 37676, framed by some delightful small craft moored in the tiny harbour of Golant on the River Fowey at high tide, makes for Carne Point with clay loads during July 1999. By this time the days of Class 37 operation in Cornwall were numbered. JAMV

dedicated sidings. However, other than for the original lines of the Cornwall Minerals Railway most of this development was piecemeal. It must be remembered that Cornish roads were poor and lumbering carts with a three-ton capacity were an inefficient and costly method of conveying clay from pit to port. China clay by rail was the only practical solution to the transportation problem.

Over the years hundreds of small independent clay companies were established leading to fragmented transportation arrangements. It took until the 20th century for many producers to realise the potential benefits of operating under 'economy of scale' principles and this resulted in a series of takeovers. It must be remembered that the annual production of some of the smaller pits was less than a single modern trainload of 1,250 tonnes. In the long term the mighty English China Clay Company (ECC) dominated with over 100 small companies being absorbed within its corporate umbrella.

Technology played an important part in the development of the industry. Pipeline and pumping technology improved out of all recognition and it became possible to transport china clay in liquid slurry form many miles, resulting in clay drying installations being located many miles from the clay pit source.

By the end of the Victorian era the age of the small wooden sailing ship was coming to an end resulting in the abandonment of many small harbours, such as Pentewan and Newquay, which could not accommodate larger steam ships. In addition to outbound clay, coal was imported in large volumes to fire the boilers and engines used in the pits and dries. However, other forms of energy gradually became

available resulting in the closure of the old coal fired kilns, although the last example continued in service until 1989. Kiln closures also resulted in larger and centralised drying plants, with a consequent reduction in the railway network. The railway companies were obliged to adapt to these various changes.

By the time the railways were Nationalised in 1948 the Cornish china clay scene substantially comprised a single carrier, British Railways, meeting the requirements of a single customer, English China Clays (although the independent Goonvean company made limited use of rail transport). By the early 1960s diesel traction had replaced steam and in terms of shipping the ports of Fowey and Par (which had both been developed over the years) handled 99 percent of traffic. Most of Cornwall's so called 'white gold' was still conveyed in small 20-ton gross wooden bodied vacuum braked wagons, some of which were called 'clay hoods' due to a tent shaped frame for the tarpaulin covers that protected the china clay from the elements and contamination. The last of these wagons was built at Swindon in 1960 and it was only a matter of time before they would require replacement.

It should perhaps be mentioned for completeness that in the past china clay and ball clay were also transported by rail in the County of Devon and in Dorset. Nearest to Cornwall was the clay drying installation at Marsh Mills, to the east of Plymouth. China clay was piped from Lee Moor for drying but sadly rail traffic to Marsh Mills, via Tavistock Junction, ceased a few years ago. Clay traffic also entered Cornwall from a plant on the Heathfield branch, near Newton Abbot, and clay was transported by rail in North Devon in the Meeth and Marland area.

The 1960s, 1970s and 1980s were not kind in terms of the 'china clay by rail' map. Branches and sidings closed in many areas, the main examples being Wenford Bridge, Parkandillack to St Dennis Junction, the Retew branch, the Goonbarrow branch, the Carbis branch, the Wheal Rose branch, Drinnick Mill lower, the Bojea branch and St Blazey to Fowey, the latter being converted to a road for the exclusive use of ECC lorries travelling to and from Fowey. The docks there would continue to be accessed by rail but via Lostwithiel. It should be remembered that some of these closed branch lines had well over a dozen individual clay kilns located along their route. Even in the 1990s the decline continued with clay drying installations at Moorswater and Ponts Mill closing.

ECC was a profitable company and their large headquarters building at St Austell dominated that part of the town. However, mineral production in Cornwall has always been susceptible to the vagaries of the world's commodity markets and just as the world copper prices crashed in the 1860s and the price of iron ore plummeted in the 1870s, forcing thousands of Cornishmen to emigrate, the price of china clay increasingly came under pressure as vast deposits were exploited in other countries by the use of cheap labour, especially Brazil.

Any reduction in output obviously affected not only ECC but also BR. In February 1988 nearly 500 old clay hood wagons were pensioned off and most were subsequently scrapped at Sharpness Docks. These old vacuum braked short wheelbase wagons had a tare of only 13 tons and were limited to 45mph. Modernisation comprised new air braked roller

Left: St Blazey Yard was once the transportation hub for 'china clay by rail' movements. There was a locomotive stabling point, a shunter allocation, refuelling equipment, a wagon works and a central office where everything from wagon and train movements to crew and locomotive rostering were managed. Gradually its importance diminished as the china clay industry contracted. By 2008 the location resembled a ghost town, largely devoid of wagons and with EWS locomotives stabled at Carne Point, Fowey overnight. The only activity was the short term stabling of complete trains. In this September 1998 view all three classes of motive power then employed on clay trains in Cornwall are featured, before the arrival of Class 66s. With shunter No. 08953 in the foreground, No. 60006 Scunthorpe Ironmaster, a rare visitor in livery terms, propels a dead Class 37 No. 37521 towards the shed. JAMV

bearing CDA wagons, a development of the well known HAA merry-go-round hopper discharge coal wagons. Initially 124 examples were procured but this number was later increased. When fully loaded these wagons had a gross weight of 50 tonnes, the payload element being 33 tonnes of china clay. In the 1980s long distance china clay hauls within the UK and to Europe also had a new generation of bogie wagons made available including Polybulks, PBA 'Tigers', TCA tankers and several four wheel examples including PAA, PRA, VDA, VGA etc.

The motive power scene also changed. Following the demise of diesel-hydraulic Classes 22, 41, 42, 43 and 52 between 1967 and 1977 diesel-electric locomotives arrived in the Royal Duchy. Lighter duties were handled by Class 25s, imported from the London Midland Region, other work being handled by Type 4 motive power, mainly Classes 45, 46 'Peak' locos and 47s. Some domestic traffic in Cornwall was hauled by the larger locomotives but their primary role was heading the long distance air braked services. On occasions pairs of the smaller Type 2 locomotives would work in multiple. Probably the most notable Cornish motive power event was when the first Class 37s were imported. The first of the class to work domestic china clay trains in the county

was in 1978 and for over 20 years these reliable locomotives ruled the roost. The humble shunter should not be forgotten, the mainstay over the decades being Class 08 but with Classes 04, 09 and 10 also finding employment, especially at St Blazey and Fowey Docks

Type 4 locomotives continued to work 'up country' on the heavier long-distance trains but Classes 45 and 46 were banned west of Bristol in October 1985. By 1974/75 Class 50 diesel-electrics had arrived in Cornwall, again from the LMR, and although primarily used on class 1 passenger trains, occasionally, especially if a locomotive was on test following fault rectification at Plymouth Laira depot, these 100mph thoroughbreds could be found working humble clay trains. Eventually double-headed Class 37s were used on some of the long distance trains but at a cost. An interesting experiment occurred between 1987 and 1989 when a single Class 50 locomotive was converted for freight use in Cornwall, No. 50049 *Defiance* becoming No. 50149. While not a complete failure the experiment was not perpetuated, reconversion taking place in 1989. In order to dispense with expensive double-headed Class 37 operations a trial was conducted in 1990 using a 3,250hp Class 56 locomotive. Clearance tests and other trials were conducted on 27 February 1990

but again the matter was not pursued as Class 60 locomotives had begun to appear on the network. However, it would be 1995 before that class regularly appeared in the county. They eventually took over most long distance trains including the famous 'Silver Bullet' clay slurry haul between Burngullow and the Caledonian Paper Company at Irvine in Scotland, at the time the longest freight haul in the UK.

In the meantime BR had been playing games with its corporate structure, mindful all the while that political influence was being brought to bear to make sectors of the loss making railways more accountable. In succession the freight operations in Cornwall were placed under a locally managed 'Cornish Railways' structure in 1984. A Railfreight organisation was subsequently created and this was divided into sub-sectors such as distribution, construction, coal, metals and petroleum. This was followed by the creation of three shadow privatised limited companies, with china clay operations falling under the 'Transrail' label, which was formally launched in Cornwall on 9 September 1994.

This was really the warm up act for the full privatisation of the railways a couple of years later. Under a bidding arrangement expressions of interest were invited and to the surprise of

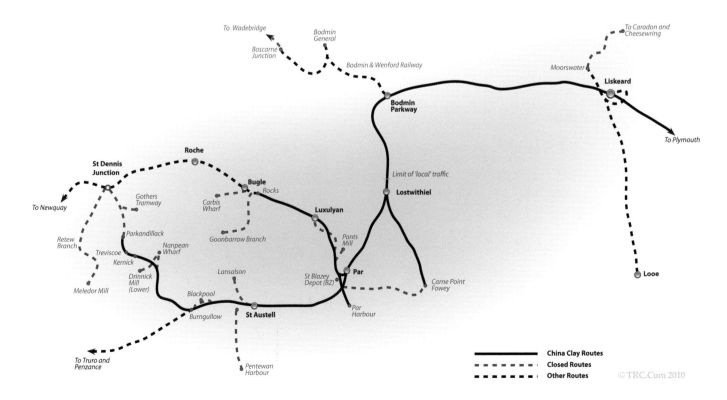

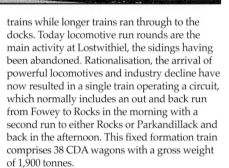

Above: *As soon as the North American-owned company received the news that they had won a major UK freight franchise, they reviewed the motive power they inherited and immediately embarked on a major new build procurement, based on a precedent established in the Class 59 design of the mid-1980s. EWS ordered 250 high-tech computer controlled locomotives from General Motors. The first example to arrive in Cornwall was No. 66027, which hauled its first china clay train on 9 January 1999. Looking stunning in its brand new 'out of the box' livery No. 66123 negotiates the curves on the approach to Luxulyan on the Newquay branch with empty CDAs for the Rocks works at Goonbarrow Junction, in July 1999. JAMV*

Right: *One of the original vacuum-braked 'clay-hood' wagons No. B743000 in immaculate ex works condition with clean bodywork and blue ECC hood tarpulin. CJM*

some it was the North American Wisconsin Central Railway that was successful. They started trading under the name of English Welsh & Scottish Railways, shown as EW&S and later just plain EWS on its locomotives. With its North American links it was perhaps hardly surprising that the company ordered powerful new build high-tech General Motors (GM) locomotives. This resulted in Class 66s arriving in Cornwall in 1999, gradually replacing all other classes. In this crazy world of global finance and multi-national companies EWS was subsequently acquired by DB Schenker, a subsidiary of Deutsche Bahn (alias German Railways).

As regards ECC, trading in the 1990s continued to decline and the total value of the company by share price resulted in the company becoming a target of the French company Imetal, later known as Imerys. In 1999 the unthinkable happened when ECC was acquired by its French rival for £756m. Imerys has international interests in 250 mining and other extractive industry sites in 47 countries and it has proved possible to source china clay more cheaply overseas. From 5,500 ECC employees in 1976 this reduced to 4,000 in 1996, 2,000 in 2006 with a current Imerys target of only 1,300 staff, a massive reduction in percentage terms. The human impact has been considerable with the company offering legal,

financial and stress counselling for redundant staff.

The decline continued with the massive Blackpool installation at Burngullow closing at the end of 2007 with 800 redundancies, the nearby Crugwallins clay dries also closed and the famous 'Silver Bullet' ceased to run.

Unbelievably in 2008, after 175 years of operation, the shipment of china clay from Par Harbour ceased and all ships were diverted to Fowey. In April 2009 a complete halt in the production of china clay was implemented for a period of one calendar month. In 2009 Imerys signed a 5 year contract with EWS (now DB Schenker) for the carriage of china clay by rail. Imerys has a green policy of moving as much china clay by rail as possible, thereby reducing carbon emissions, but it is the volume that is paramount to railfans.

In recent years gone by there were a dozen or so daily clay trains operating in Cornwall from a large number of loading points. The main ones since the end of the 1990s being Rocks works at Goonbarrow Junction on the Newquay branch line, Blackpool at Burngullow and Kernick, Trelavour and Parkandillack on the Drinnick Mill branch. Local traffic was all focused on Lostwithiel where the wagons would be tripped down to Carne Point at Fowey for unloading.

Sometimes wagons would be deposited in sidings at Lostwithiel and combined with other

trains while longer trains ran through to the docks. Today locomotive run rounds are the main activity at Lostwithiel, the sidings having been abandoned. Rationalisation, the arrival of powerful locomotives and industry decline have now resulted in a single train operating a circuit, which normally includes an out and back run from Fowey to Rocks in the morning with a second run to either Rocks or Parkandillack and back in the afternoon. This fixed formation train comprises 38 CDA wagons with a gross weight of 1,900 tonnes.

On the long distance scene dedicated block trains to Europe have ceased. From a position where at least two air braked trains of china clay left the county every day the only surviving block load is to Stoke-on-Trent and that has been reduced to a weekly service, with most of the clay being loaded in JIA bogie hoppers. Some of these wagons are loaded at Par Harbour, normally once per week. Whereas 70 per cent of all china clay is used in the production of paper the train to Cliffe Vale, Stoke-on-Trent is a 'pottery' train, serving an industry that is also in decline. Wagonload, Speedlink and Enterprise activities died some time ago. All of this contraction has had a disastrous impact on the railways of Cornwall with St Blazey being all but closed and the EWS/DB locomotive(s) being stabled at Carne Point overnight. The massive Burngullow site is now used only for wagon storage and in Devon even Tavistock Junction yard has now closed. Overall the scene is somewhat depressing.

For the foreseeable future there will still be a china clay industry in Cornwall and indeed some inward investment has been made by Imerys but mainly to perform existing activities more efficiently, with little prospect of an increase in rail traffic or manpower. For example there has been a move from wet to energy saving dry mining. Presently Cornish china clay production is about 1.4 million tons per annum, which is exported to 60 countries. For the railfan the great days have, sadly, gone forever. We now have a German Company moving clay for a French company with American locomotives. Whatever happened to British Railways and English China Clay? ∎

Left Top: *The new order of the day in Cornish clay transport, the air braked CDA four-wheel hopper car with a roller tilt hood. These vehicles were based on the MGR coal hopper and were introduced from 1987, with a total of 123 wagons currently in the clay pool. No. 375027 is illustrated at Lostwithiel on 9 April 1995. CJM*

Left Middle: *Not only has local Cornish china clay traffic reduced in recent times but the long distance hauls have almost disappeared. Not so long ago there were long haul Polybulk workings to Switzerland and Italy, as well as block loads of clay slurry from Burngullow to Irvine in Scotland (the UK's longest freight haul), pelletised clay to Cliffe Vale, Stoke-on-Trent as well as multifarious wagonloads to a wide range of customers. All have now gone except the now weekly train to Stoke. Here in June 1997 the famous Burngullow to Irvine 'Silver Bullet' is seen crossing Bolitho Viaduct with ten bogie wagons behind Class 60 No. 60062 Samuel Johnson. This traffic flow commenced in 1989 and by 1999 over 1 million tonnes had been transported. The service was axed in 2007 with the clay being sourced in Brazil. JAMV*

Below: *Par station is now the best location in Cornwall to observe china clay trains because traffic from both the Fowey and Drinnick Mill branches visit the station area. There is a useful road overbridge and footbridge for viewing or photography, the delightful semaphore signals give good notice of an approaching train on all lines, it is the junction for Newquay, there are protective awnings and if absolutely nothing happens there is always the Royal Oak pub adjacent to the station. Having just brought a heavy load of bogie wagons up from Burngullow and having run round its train Class 66 No. 66074 propels its wagons clear of the station before continuing to St Blazey yard, in September 2004. JAMV*

Right: The Drinnick Mill branch from Burngullow to Parkandillack via Kernick and Treviscoe is still an important china clay line, even though a mere shadow of earlier years. Dozens of minor clay kilns along the branch have been closed and currently the line normally attracts just a single train of CDAs per day, although when the Stoke-on-Trent wagons are being delivered/collected the tally can double. In September 2002 No. 66239 is seen passing the site of Rostowrack siding near Slip Bridge with JIA and PBA wagons for the Potteries. Note the massive clay tips in the background. JAMV

Below: Although china clay train traffic levels have declined during the past decade there is still immense attraction in the total railway environment in which such trains operate. Cornwall still has seven manual signalboxes (four on the clay 'circuit') that control lower quadrant semaphore signals, there is some splendid railway infrastructure, single line working and tokens, causeways, crossing gates, great viaducts and scenic river valleys in the magnificent Cornish countryside, all waiting to be explored. The only photographic requirements are patience, a decent camera and fair weather. Here the Lostwithiel signalman is handing over the single line token for the Fowey branch to the driver of No. 66019 in October 2007. There are five semaphore signals visible in this shot, all in the 'on' position. JAMV

Above: *1999 turned out to be a very significant year for the Cornish china clay industry when to the surprise of many the long established English China Clay Company was taken over by its French rival Imetal (later named Imerys). ECC was acquired for what many considered to be a modest £756m. Thus EWS found themselves working with a new customer. One of the main ECC/Imerys works is Rocks at Goonbarrow Junction, an inaccessible location for the general public. With the works sidings in the foreground other items of interest are the old GWR signalbox with its semaphore signals, the red ex-Post Office K2 telephone box and a shiny No. 66123, returning light engine to St Blazey. JAMV*

Left Middle: *As described in the text, the china clay story in Cornwall during the past decade has been one of decline, with many installations being closed and associated rail traffic reduced. When combined with a policy of rationalisation and centralisation and an international commodities situation where china clay has been sourced from other countries the future has at times looked bleak. With the closure of Marsh Mills and Heathfield in Devon as well as Moorswater clay dries there are now no 'local' CDA wagon movements east of Lostwithiel! In this July 1999 view an IC125 train is unusually delayed at Saltash for westbound china clay loads to pass. Hauled by No. 66120 the ex-Marsh Mills wagons are leaving the single line across the Royal Albert Bridge bound for Carne Point, Fowey. JAMV*

Left Bottom: *If ever a photograph summed up the decline of the Cornish china clay industry this must be it. Having closed towards the end of 2007 this view shows the abandoned clay dries at Crugwallins, near Burngullow. The last train has departed, the drying machinery has been stripped out, the last employee has long gone and the linhay is silent and desolate. This site has now been secured and fenced-off. JAMV*

Above: When this photograph was taken of Blackpool dries at Burngullow featuring No. 66207 shunting in October 2006, the writing was on the wall for some aspects of the Cornish china clay industry. Production volumes were declining prior to the recession that occurred during 2008/9. This remarkable busy site was modernised by ECC during 1988/89, the company spending over £2m on changes to infrastructure and track layout. To the shock of many the vast site and its associated clay pit and works closed at the end of 2007 with a loss of 800 jobs. Now it is hard to believe that the entire site is used only for wagon storage, except for one siding where Freightliner sand trains are loaded. JAMV

Above: On 13 April 2007, EWS No. 66137 slowly pulls off the Parkandillack line at Burngullow with a clay train from Treviscoe. After recessing in Burngullow yard the train worked forward to St Blazey and then formed part of an evening freight departure to Newport. CJM

Night Photography

By Colin J. Marsden

The photography of trains at night can be very rewarding, with some excellent results obtained. In the days of film cameras, a good strong shake resistant tripod was needed, with a cable release. In those days a photographer on a station in the dark hours with a camera was not deemed a national security risk and were usually left alone by station staff and police.

Some quite long exposures were needed to record quality images, frequently using the black and white medium. On a personal note, I used Tri-X or later XP2 rated at 400ASA and in a good brightish station used about 10sec at *f*8 as a starting point, if in doubt other exposures either side of that would be made and hopefully when developed the results were satisfactory.

With the increased use of colour, either slide or print film, the exposure was far more critical and hand held light meters or some state-of-the-art through the lens (TTL) metering assisted in the required result.

With colour, the light balance had to be left to the recording ability of the film, with adjustments made on the enlarging easel for prints and just had to be accepted for colour slides.

The onset of the digital photographic era opened up a new field in night railway photography. Once the early pre-set cameras had been superseded by high-quality cameras mainly manufactured by Nikon and Canon, and the problems of long exposure of high ISO speed had been overcome, huge advances on night and low light railway image recording were possible.

Exposure was again critical, but the ability to edit images on a computer screen rather than in a wet dark room allowed some fine adjustments of dark and light areas.

As digital cameras have evolved, and the ability to record images using high ISO speeds has emerged, it has now become possible on some of the high-end cameras from both the leading manufacturers to record images at up to 6400ISO without problems, allowing the taking of even moving trains in the dark hours. This has become especially useful at a time when the erection of tripods on station platforms is frowned upon.

However, high ISO recording is not always the answer, this can cause colour fringing on bright subjects, poor colour representation and sometimes flat images.

If it is at all possible it is recommended to use a recording speed of 100-200ISO for night exposures and adjust the time the camera is 'open'. The table on the right shows the authors guide to night exposure using a Nikon D700 camera. (The 100ISO represents using a low ISO setting).

The problems with colour cast or white balance have been largely addressed with digital photography. The white balance can be adjusted on either the camera under the white balance setting - increasing the white balance figure will 'warm' up (make reder) the image, by reducing the figure the image will get cooler (bluer). White balance can also be adjusted on the computer if you took your images in a raw setting, much the same adjustment as on the camera can be made. But a word of advice, try and keep the image colour looking correct.

In the main the equipment for todays night shoot has altered little from years ago. A good high quality sturdy tripod (with a level if possible), an electronic cable release and patience are the main required items. Then go out and shoot, try for yourself, experiment with short, medium and long exposures and by altering the white balance. It costs nothing to take a digital image. ■

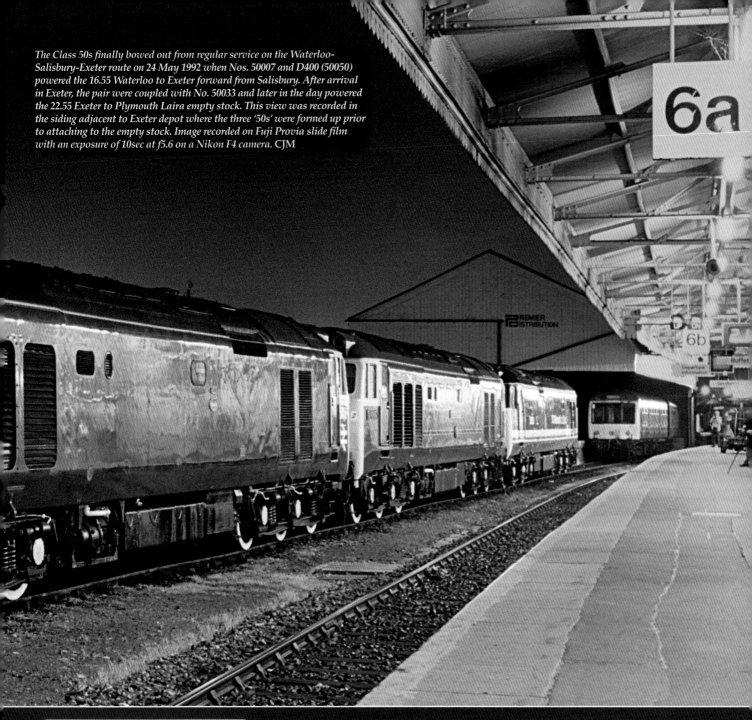

The Class 50s finally bowed out from regular service on the Waterloo-Salisbury-Exeter route on 24 May 1992 when Nos. 50007 and D400 (50050) powered the 16.55 Waterloo to Exeter forward from Salisbury. After arrival in Exeter, the pair were coupled with No. 50033 and later in the day powered the 22.55 Exeter to Plymouth Laira empty stock. This view was recorded in the siding adjacent to Exeter depot where the three '50s' were formed up prior to attaching to the empty stock. Image recorded on Fuji Provia slide film with an exposure of 10sec at f5.6 on a Nikon F4 camera. CJM

6a

Night Exposure Fact File

Exposure comparison - The following exposure will give the same light recording value, but offering a very different depth of field (f2.8 being worse and f16 being the best). It has to be a calculation between length of exposure and depth of field.

Average night station lighting		
100ISO	200ISO	400ISO
f2.8 – 2 sec	f2.8 – 1 sec	f2.8 – 0.5 sec
f4 – 4 sec	f4 – 2 sec	f4 – 1 sec
f5.6 – 8 sec	f5.6 – 4 sec	f5.6 – 2 sec
f8 – 16 sec	f8 – 8 sec	f8 – 4 sec
f11 – 32 sec	f11 – 16 sec	f11 – 8 sec
f16 – 64 sec	f16 – 32 sec	f16 – 16 sec

Low or Spot lighting		
100ISO	200ISO	400ISO
f2.8 – 5 sec	f2.8 – 2.5 sec	f2.8 – 1.25 sec
f4 – 10 sec	f4 – 5 sec	f4 – 2.5 sec
f5.6 – 20 sec	f5.6 – 10 sec	f5.6 – 5 sec
f8 – 40 sec	f8 – 20 sec	f8 – 10 sec
f11 – 80 sec	f11 – 40 sec	f11 – 20 sec
f16 – 160 sec	f16 – 64 sec	f16 – 40 sec

If it is possible a fill-in flash can help to improve the overall illumination of an image, but please be very careful where flash guns are discharged near trains, never point it towards the driving cab as a driver could easily be blinded which could cause a signal to be missed. ∎

Below: *Recorded on Kodachrome 64 slide film on 2 January 1976, Class 52 'Western' No. D1033 Western Trooper awaits departure from Paddington with the 17.45 Paddington to Westbury service. The exposure for this image was 30secs at f5.6 due to the very limited amount of light available at the country end of Paddington platform 1. Note the ghosting of the man on the right.* CJM

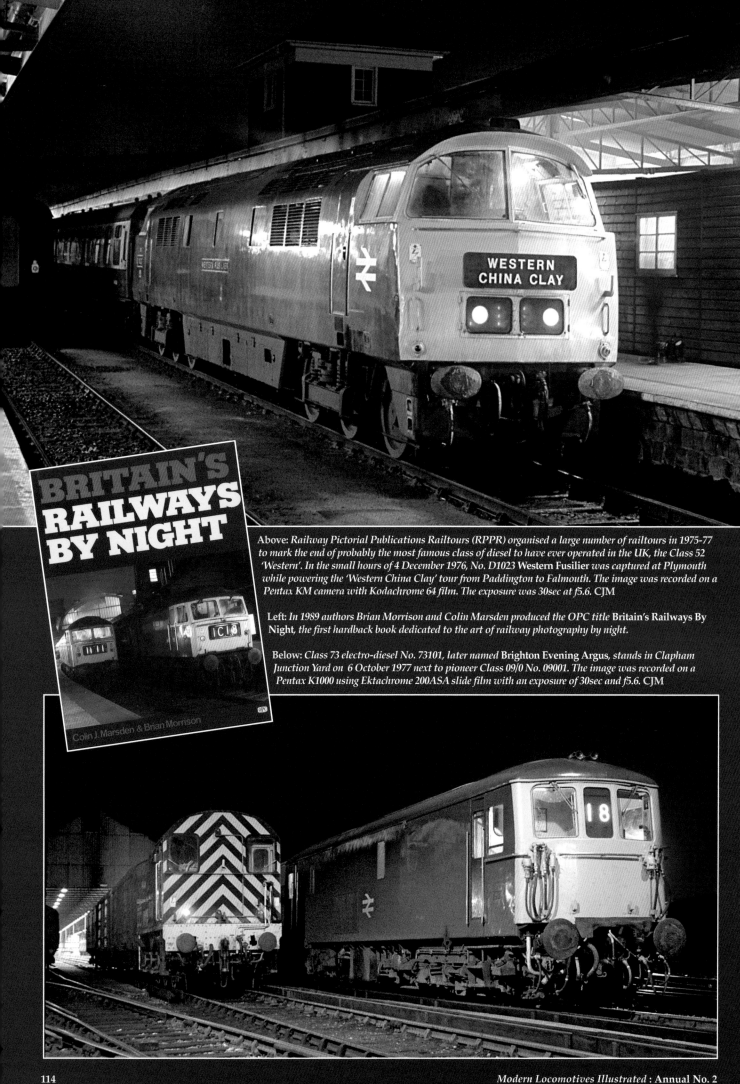

BRITAIN'S RAILWAYS BY NIGHT

Colin J. Marsden & Brian Morrison

Above: *Railway Pictorial Publications Railtours (RPPR) organised a large number of railtours in 1975-77 to mark the end of probably the most famous class of diesel to have ever operated in the UK, the Class 52 'Western'. In the small hours of 4 December 1976, No. D1023* **Western Fusilier** *was captured at Plymouth while powering the 'Western China Clay' tour from Paddington to Falmouth. The image was recorded on a Pentax KM camera with Kodachrome 64 film. The exposure was 30sec at f5.6. CJM*

Left: *In 1989 authors Brian Morrison and Colin Marsden produced the OPC title* **Britain's Railways By Night,** *the first hardback book dedicated to the art of railway photography by night.*

Below: *Class 73 electro-diesel No. 73101, later named* **Brighton Evening Argus,** *stands in Clapham Junction Yard on 6 October 1977 next to pioneer Class 09/0 No. 09001. The image was recorded on a Pentax K1000 using Ektachrome 200ASA slide film with an exposure of 30sec and f5.6. CJM*

Above: *Railway Pictorial Publications Railtours (RPPR) 'Western China Clay' tour on 4 December 1976 from Paddington to Falmouth and return, was powered back to London by No. D1056 **Western Sultan**. The train is seen below the great Brunel roof of Paddington train shed. Note the then new InterCity HST on the left. The image was recorded on a Pentax KM camera using Kodachrome 64 film. The exposure was 25sec at f5.6. CJM*

Below: *Long exposures can often produce interesting effects, especially where such items as steam are billowing around. Seen at Leeds City station on 31 January 1980, 'Peak' No. 45056 awaits departure with the 18.35 service to Carlisle. The loco's steam heating boiler is producing a wave of steam which is highlighted by the signals and station lighting, while the exposure of 30 seconds has captured the change of the signal aspect from red to green. The image was recorded on a Nikon FM2 on Kodak Ektachrome film with an exposure of 30sec at f6.3. CJM*

Above: *Night photography using black & white film often produces some excellent results with fine graduation texture and interesting lighting effects. For several years when employed as a driver on BR Southern Region, the author recorded black & white images of Southern EMUs on a Pentax 6x7 or Mamiya 645 using Kodak Tri-X film rated at 400ISO. At around 20.00 on the evening of 6 October 1981 Class 405 4SUB No. 4639 is seen in one of the bay platforms at Twickenham while forming the 19.26 Waterloo to Waterloo via Kingston parcels service. The wet platform adds considerable texture to the image. Taken on a Pentax 6x7 using Kodak Tri-X film at 400ASA. Exposure 30sec at f8.* CJM

Below: *Dual heat (steam and electric) Class 31/4 No. 31411 stands at Leeds City station in the small hours of 4 February 1983 with a rake of empty Mk1 sleeping car stock which it had powered from the nearby Neville Hill depot. The stock was to be attached to a northbound sleeper service from London to Scotland routed by way of Leeds. This Class 31 was unusual in that it carried its five digit TOPS number below each cabside window, rather than just below the drivers side window. The Leeds Dragonara hotel in the background adds a further dimension to this picture. Recorded on a Mamiya 645 on Kodak Tri-X film rated at 400ASA and scanned direct from the negative.* CJM

Above: *Even the 1980s lighting at London Waterloo was quite powerful and gave good and even illumination for night photography. Taken at 02.30 in the morning of 22 April 1981, Class 405 4SUB No. 4657 is seen stabled in the then platform 15 with stock for an early morning departure to Windsor. In platform 14 a light Class 73 can be seen. The office block to the left of this picture has now been demolished and was part of the mid-1990s Waterloo International station development. Taken on a Mamiya 645 1000S using Kodak Tri-x film rated at 400ASA. The exposure was 10sec at f8. CJM*

Below: *Bristol Temple Meads station was another hub of overnight rail activity with sleeping car services, parcels, mail and newspaper trains and several all-night passenger services. With a rake of blue and grey-liveried Mk1s behind, ETH-fitted Class 31/4 No. 31422 was recorded at Bristol Temple Meads at 23.00 on 8 June 1982 with empty stock off a Portsmouth service bound for Malago Vale carriage sidings. Image recorded on a Pentax 6x7 using Kodak Tri-x film rated at 400ASA. The exposure given was 15 sec at f6.3. CJM*

Above: The wonderful and graceful style of the Swindon-built InterCity DMUs always looked good in a picture, made even better by some interesting lighting under the Brunel roof at London Paddington. Running as London set No. L714, a Class 123 formation is seen on 2 January 1976 awaiting attachment of another like unit before forming the 18.25 Paddington to Oxford semi-fast service. Taken on a Pentax K1000 on Kodak Ektachrome 200ASA film. The exposure was 10sec at f8. CJM

Below: Taken at dusk rather than completely at night is this study at Glasgow Central on 5 June 1997 of then North of London Eurostar set No. (37)3308/07. This was the first time a Eurostar set had been in Glasgow Central station and one of the few images of a Eurostar captured in the main part of the station. The set was involved in platform gauging work for the then proposed Glasgow to Paris through daytime service. The image was recorded on a Nikon F4 using Kodak Gold 100ASA film with an exposure of 5sec at f5.6. CJM

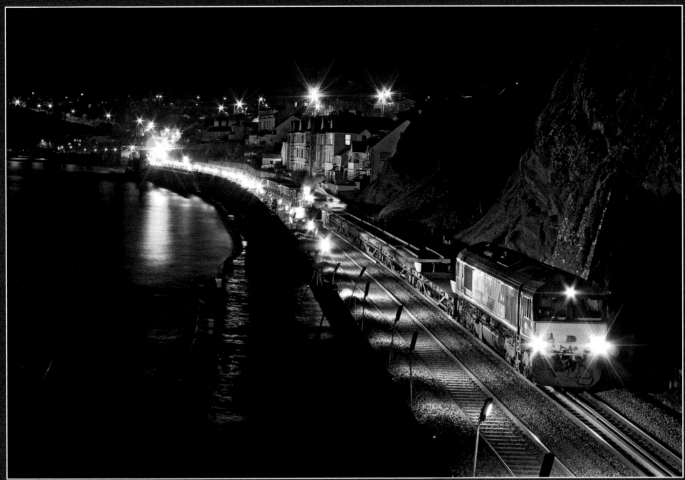

Above & Below: Track engineering work often provides for some interesting night photographs, providing the photographer can find somewhere safe to stand and the weather is not too inclement. Overnight engineering sites are usually well illuminated by temporary light supplied by a site generator. Usually this is very 'white' light and allows for some accurate exposures without much colour correction. The photographer has also to be careful that temporary lighting does not shine directly into the camera lens. In the above view, illuminated entirely by temporary lighting, DBS Class 66/0 No. 66117 is seen on the Sea Wall section between Dawlish and Dawlish Warren during the night of 14/15 February 2009 powering train 6W41, the 16.36 Westbury to Dawlish via Newton Abbot. Lights in local residences, on the track machine and loco provide some extra illumination. In the view below, the scene is enhanced by a track worker cutting through one of the tracks of the down line, providing an interesting array of sparks. Views such as this require quite a long exposure time and thus a risk exists of people moving. The exposure of the upper view, taken on a Canon 400D was 30sec at f16 with an ISO of 200, while the view below taken on the same camera, had an exposure of 25sec at f11, also at 200ISO. Both: Nathan Williamson

Above: Carlisle is a station which lends itself to night photography, sodium (yellow) lights illuminate the main train shed, while whiter lights are found on the platforms. This excellent exposure was captured on 1 April 2010 and shows failed Royal Mail Class 325 No. 325016 after it had been hauled into the station by DBS Class 66/0 No. 66107. On the right is Direct Rail Services Class 47/7 No. 47790 which later took the train south. Recorded on a Canon 50D with an exposure of 5sec at f8 with an ISO setting of 200. Tony Christie

Below: Today with high-end digital cameras it is quite possible to pump up the ISO speed and capture images after dark without the need of a tri-pod, this feature is especially useful if one has to travel light. This image recorded at 20.00 at Los Angeles Union station on 1 March 2007 shows a Gold Line Metro Rail service and was taken hand held on a Nikon D2X with an ISO of 800 giving an exposure of 1/25 of a sec at f2.8. The lens used was a 50mm f1.4 prime. CJM

Above: *The companion view to the image reproduced opposite at Carlisle, is taken from the opposite platform and shows the DRS Class 47 attached to the front of the Royal Mail set. The image was recorded on a Canon 50D with an exposure of 5sec at f8 with an ISO setting of 200.* Tony Christie

Below: *With the introduction of the Nikon D3 and D700 series cameras, night photography took a major step forward, with the ability to capture good reproduceable pictures at very high ISO settings, with up to 6400ISO providing usable images. This view of a Class 159 at Dawlish taken on 12 December 2009 used an ISO setting of 3200 which allowed the picture to be taken in full night light at 1/100 sec at f2. The camera used was a Nikon D700 with a 50mm f1.4 set to f2. The image was taken in Nikon raw (NEF) and processed in Nikon Capture then Photoshop CS4.* CJM

On the Drawing Board

By Colin J. Marsden

Over the years a considerable number of train designs have been put on the Drawing Board of either railway owned or private drawing offices. Many of the pen and ink or even medium scale models have been refined into production locomotives, multiple units and carriages, but a significant number have ended up in the bin.

Thankfully a number of these early artists impressions and models have survived and were frequently used as press pack illustrative material for new train announcements or plans for proposed new services.

Under the control of Chris Green, the BR London & South East operating business Network South East were experts at producing sketches and even full size mock-ups of new train designs, frequently with speculative class numbers and revised liveries.

This included some early pre-production drawings of the Class 159 DMUs to replace loco hauled stock on the Waterloo to Exeter route and several different mock ups and drawings for various 'Networker' EMUs for the Kent line modernisation programme, this saw several different front end designs which culminated in a much revised form used in the building of the Class 465 and 375 sets, the Class 375s at the time being referred to as Class 471.

The east-west London 'CrossRail' project which at one time came under the NSE banner in the late 1980s saw several mock-ups of a proposed Class 341, which was displayed on the concourse at London Paddington station, perhaps this was a little premature with the project still awaiting commencement.

With privatisation of the UK railways from the mid 1990s, came many new train design artists impressions and mock-ups. Some of the most impressive were produced by the Virgin empire for their franchise of the West Coast main line, where long prior to the announcement of the final Pendolino design, a press brief in London surrounded some very stylish train design models, which were eventually refined into the Pendolino, while mock up of train interiors and artists impressions showed much artists licence, with a very impressive first class passenger environment, a far cry from the cramped claustrophobic interior of the finished train.

In the 1980s considerable specification and design work was placed on the Advanced Multiple Unit (AMU) project at the Railway Technical Centre, Derby. This included an exterior state-of-the-art design for a multi-powered unit with differing interiors for suburban, outer suburban and main line travel. Massive advances were also planned for the driving cab design. Sadly none of this came to fruition under the AMU banner, but much has been perpetuated into new builds by Bombardier, Siemens and Alstom. ∎

Above: *How the production Deltic might have looked if the design company Wilkes & Ashmore had their way. Following the decision to build a fleet of production 'Deltic' locos, the BTC Design Panel frowned upon the US styling of the prototype loco and directed Wilkes and Ashmore to produce a more acceptable looking design. The eventually incorporated a raked back nose end, four character route display and train name panel on the front end, a nose mounted air intake and curved windows. The production design was somewhat refined but the livery style remained much the same.*

Left: *This amazing design for a high-powered freight loco emerged from the BTC/BR Design Panel in 1969 after the plan was put forward to build a sizeable fleet of new generation freight locos with a 6,000hp output, with multiple unit passenger trains and if needed special design passenger locos with light axle loads. This futuristic loco design did not go any further than the drawing board and the production of a wooden model for discussion purposes. It is interesting to see the two level route indicator display and the early concept of light clusters*

Above: *In the mid-1980s BR were interested in obtaining a new batch of medium output shunting and trip freight locos with an output of up to 1,000hp, much in keeping with many European and North American operators of the period. Thomas Hill of Rotherham produced a full working specification complete with this drawing of a proposed 1,000hp 0-4-0 'Senatur' loco which could be fitted for ac/dc operation or have a hydraulic transmission. Sadly nothing came of the proposal.*

Below: *In the late 1980s it was proposed to turn the redundant Battersea Power Station site into an entertainment complex with a private consortium operating three 'Battersea bullet' trains between London Victoria and an off-loading platform within the complex. The BRE Industrial Design Group produced detailed plans for three 4-car Class 447 EMU sets to operate the service, having a very futuristic front end design. As the trains would have been privately owned, they were allocated coach numbers in the 99xxx series (99469-99481). The financial recession of the early 1990s saw the power station entertainment project abandoned and the trains never built. This drawing was provided for the press launch of the project.*

Left Top: In 1971 the Design Panel produced a specification for a new generation of sliding door suburban unit, which was later refined into the PEP development sets used on the Southern Region which led to the development of the Class 313, 314, 315, 507 and 508 production builds. This early model of the proposed train shows a very PEP looking front end with route code display taking the place of the non-driving front window. Note that the intermediate passenger coach had three pairs of bi-parting sliding doors.

Left: In the period prior to the announcement of rail privatisation, new trains for the Glasgow area were sought with Birmingham-based Metro-Cammell putting forward the Class 157 design as a follow-on from their successful Class 156 product. The sets would have been part of the 'Sprinter' family and primarily operated on Strathclyde services, hence this drawing carried the Strathclyde orange livery. With privatisation looming the project was never furthered and eventually the Strathclyde area of Scotland had Class 170 Bombardier built 'Turbostar' trains.

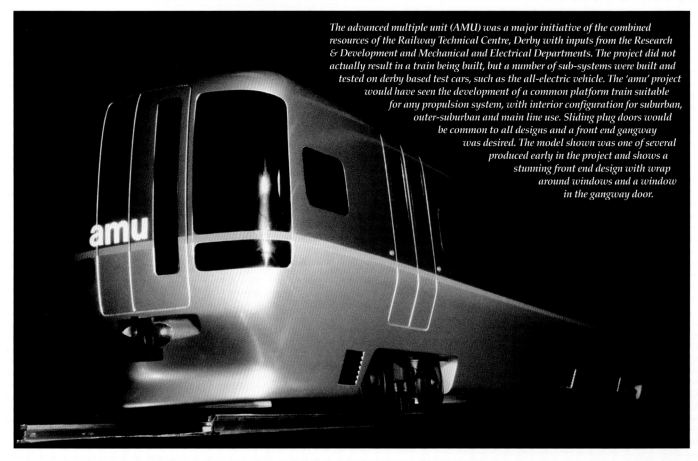

The advanced multiple unit (AMU) was a major initiative of the combined resources of the Railway Technical Centre, Derby with inputs from the Research & Development and Mechanical and Electrical Departments. The project did not actually result in a train being built, but a number of sub-systems were built and tested on derby based test cars, such as the all-electric vehicle. The 'amu' project would have seen the development of a common platform train suitable for any propulsion system, with interior configuration for suburban, outer-suburban and main line use. Sliding plug doors would be common to all designs and a front end gangway was desired. The model shown was one of several produced early in the project and shows a stunning front end design with wrap around windows and a window in the gangway door.

Above & Right: *One of the biggest train orders in modern rail history followed rail privatisation when Virgin Trains announced the total modernisation of the West Coast Main Line with a fleet of new multiple unit-based high-quality trains. Numerous press calls were held by Virgin to pave the way for the train order, with the concept drawing above produced jointly with Alstom to show how the Pendolino might look, a number of refinements were made to the finished product - perhaps this would have been a more impressive shape? The media machine of Virgin produced this interior concept drawing of how the first class would look on a Pendolino, at the time the public and press were persuaded to believe that luxury angled wood veneer chairs would be incorporated in the finished product, how wrong they were when this is compared with the cramped first class of the actual production train. Yes it would have been costly to have produced such a luxury interior, but if even just one coach of each set had been furnished in this way and a surcharge made it would have provided one of the highest quality coach interiors ever seen on a train.*

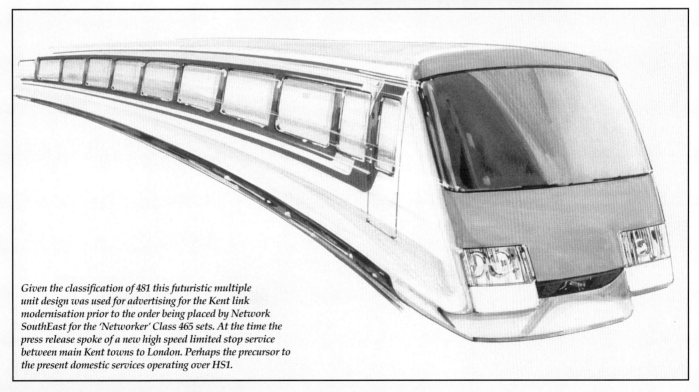

Given the classification of 481 this futuristic multiple unit design was used for advertising for the Kent link modernisation prior to the order being placed by Network SouthEast for the 'Networker' Class 465 sets. At the time the press release spoke of a new high speed limited stop service between main Kent towns to London. Perhaps the precursor to the present domestic services operating over HS1.

Above, Left & Below: *One of the largest challenges of Network South East when it took over the London and SouthEast networks in 1982 was the modernisation of the then loco-hauled Waterloo - Salisbury - Exeter route. Various options were studied including refurbishment of locos and stock, but eventually it was agreed that a follow-on order for Class 158 DMUs would be built at Derby in a three-car form dedicated for the route. These would be classified as Class 159 and able to operate in three, six or nine-car formations. The requirement was for a much high-quality interior than the then Class 158s with extra sound proofing and improved fittings. The image above is an early NSE vision of the finished train based on the then Class 158 drawings. The image left shows how the finished product turned out with set No. 159004 seen at Rosyth. The view below shows one of the drawings used in the procurement tender pack and is very similar to the actual finished train. These sets were all fully built at Derby and then sent to Rosyth Navel Base in Scotland to be fitted out by Babcock Rail.*

Right: *The Network SouthEast 'Networker' design, given the classification of Class 465 and 466 emerged in a number of drawings as Class 457 at a time when considerations were being given to building further sets of the design for use on other NSE South Thames routes, this was of course stopped by looming privatisation.*

Below: *British Rails InterCity 250 project was one of the most controversial in recent times. Designed to modernise the West Coast route from London to Birmingham, Manchester, Liverpool and Scotland. Tenders were issued to build a fleet of IC250 stock and locomotives in March 1991, with a then proposed introduction date of 1995. The trains would have been formed of up to 10 Mk5 coaches with a Class 93 loco at one and a DVT at the other, much in the same way as the East Coast was using Class 91s and Mk4 stock. Between 24 and 40 sets were planned with the most likely builders being Siemens or GEC-Alstom. The trains would have had a top speed of 155mph. With looming privatisation the IC250 project was officially abandoned in July 1992. The model of the first four metres of the driving car were produced by Seymour Powell in 1990 to act as a design tool for the project and carried proposed IC250 livery and the loco number 93001.*

Modern LOCOMOTIVES ILLUSTRATED

ONLY £4-20 AN ISSUE

Published bimonthly and edited by Colin J. Marsden, each issue of *Modern Locomotives Illustrated* traces the full history of one class or group of smaller classes of UK diesel and electric locomotives or diesel and electric multiple unit trains.
Regular features include:

- Pictures of design, build and introduction
- High-quality colour and black & white pictures in traffic
- Full documentation on modifications and liveries
- Fully detailed cab views

- Numeric 'walk round' of the class showing equipment positions
- Preservation
- Comprehensive fleet table & names
- Competitions and reviews
- Information for modellers
. . . . and much much more

Modern Locomotives Illustrated is available from high street news agents, Ian Allan Bookshops or direct from the Publishers - The Railway Centre.Com Ltd, PO Box 45, Dawlish, Devon. EX7 9XY. Or call the order line on 01626 862320.

A subscription service is available see our website www.modern-locoillustrated.com

Back issues are available at £5.20 each including post & packing.

TheRailwayCentre.Com Publishing